Backstage Girls

words & drawings – Serena Czarnecki

photographs – Annie Sprinkle & Steve Zambrano

with additional photographs by Serena Czarnecki,
Paul Johnston & Baron Wolman

edited by – Catherine Gigante-Brown
designed by – Vinnie Corbo

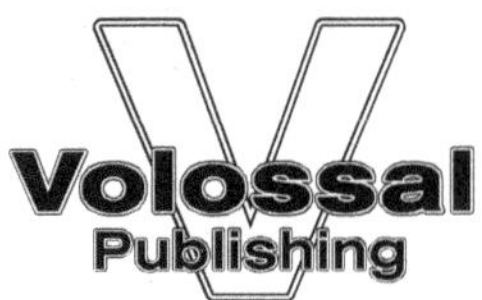

Published by Volossal Publishing
www.volossal.com

ISBN 978-0-9996916-6-3

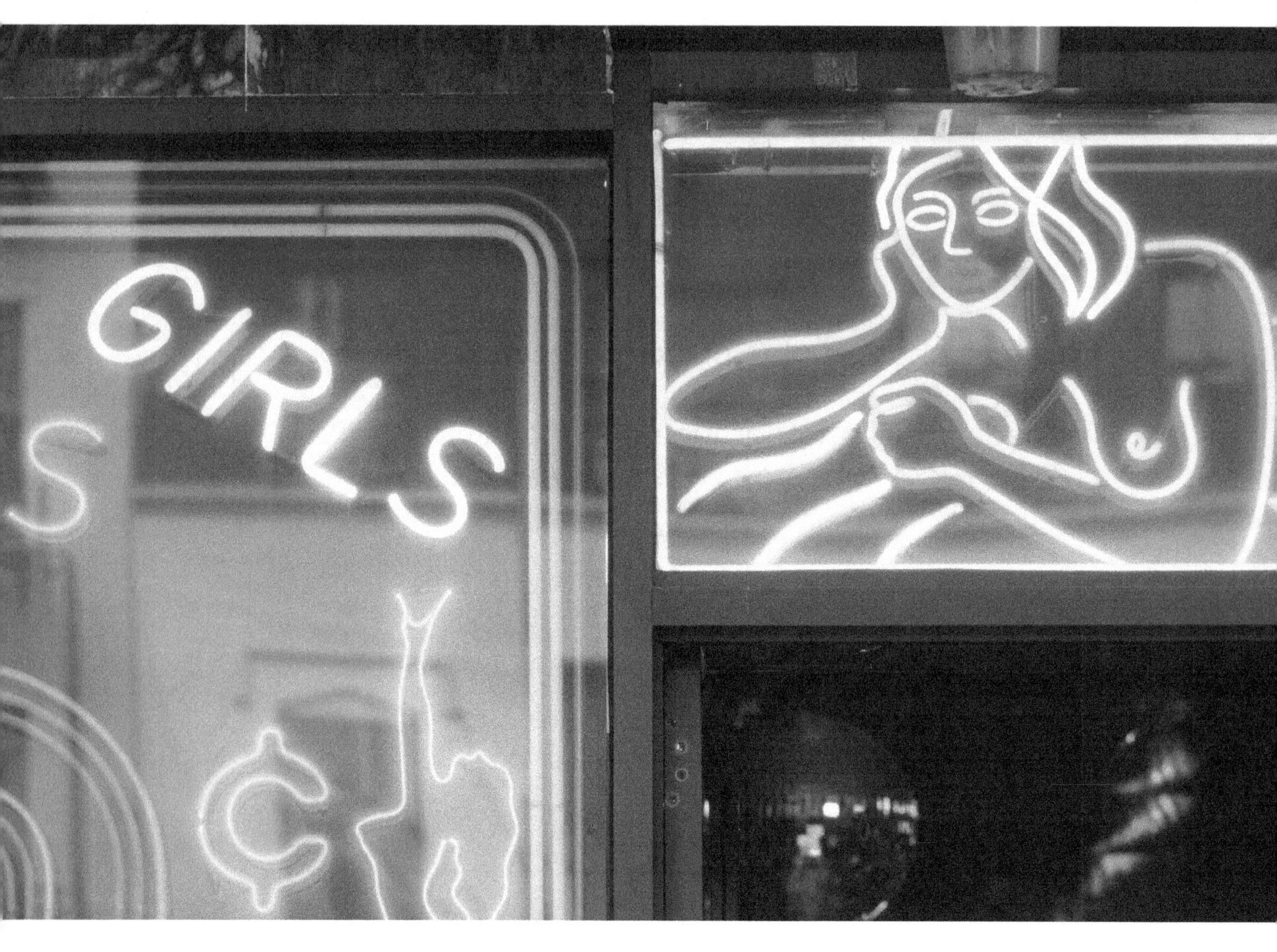
GIRLS

Table of Contents

Table of Contents

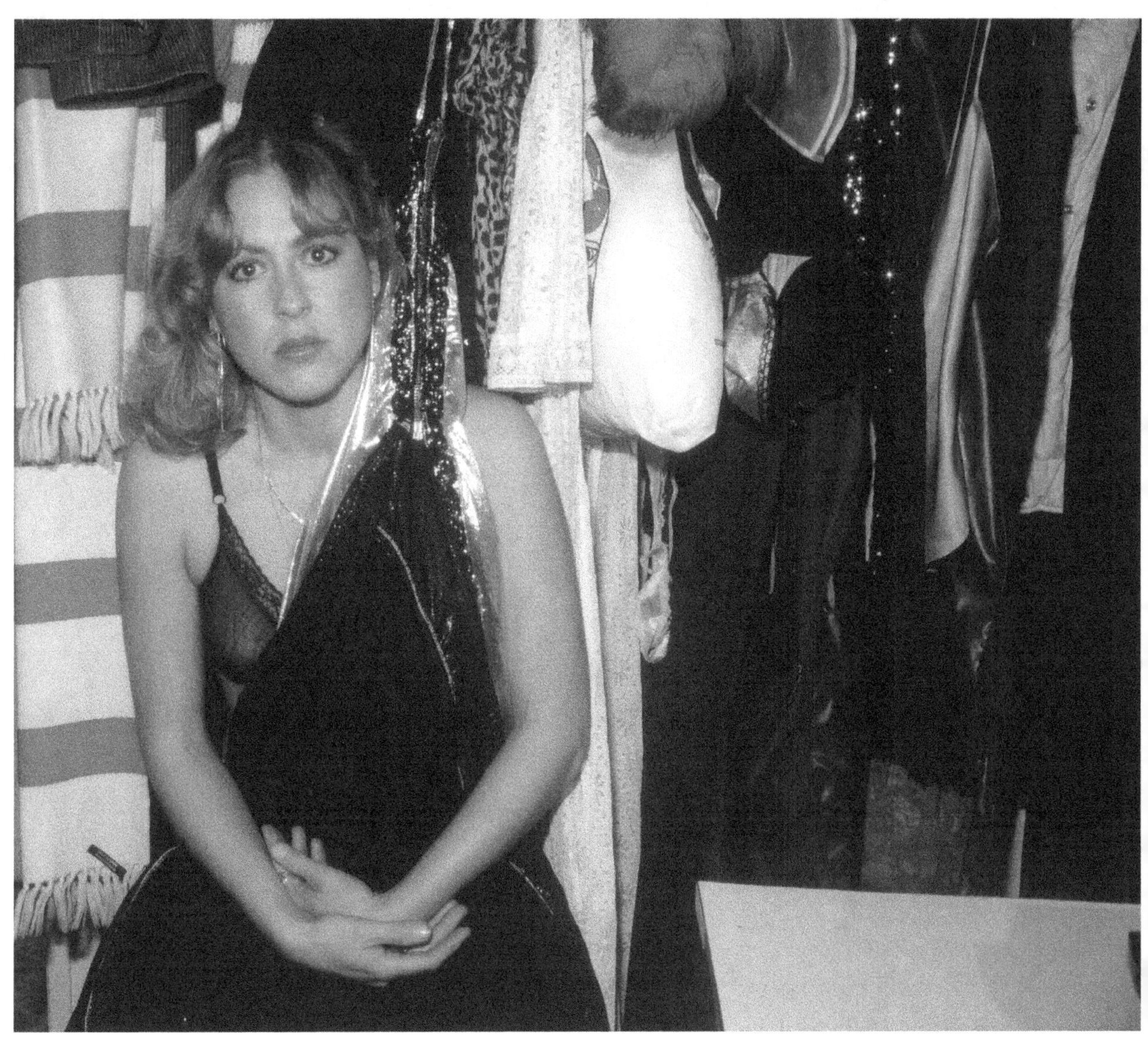

Dedication

To all the girls,
everywhere

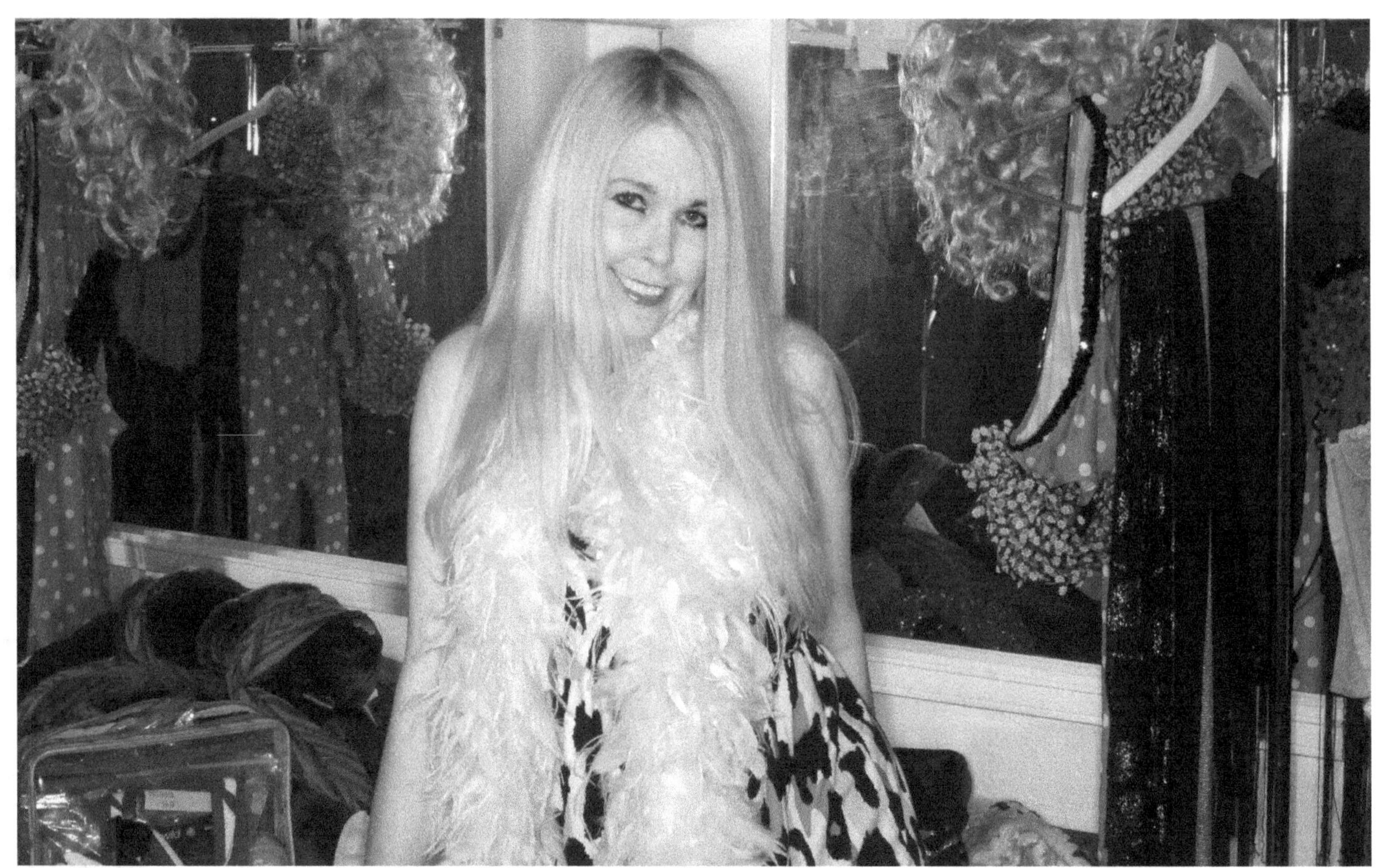

Prelude

This is what I saw.
What I heard.
Felt.

The girls were not supposed to even speak to me because I kept them from their duties.

Yet their faces lit up when my camera was near, when any camera was near—they were eager to be captured and for me to like them.

But I did more than like them. Maybe I even loved them. Even if just for a little while.

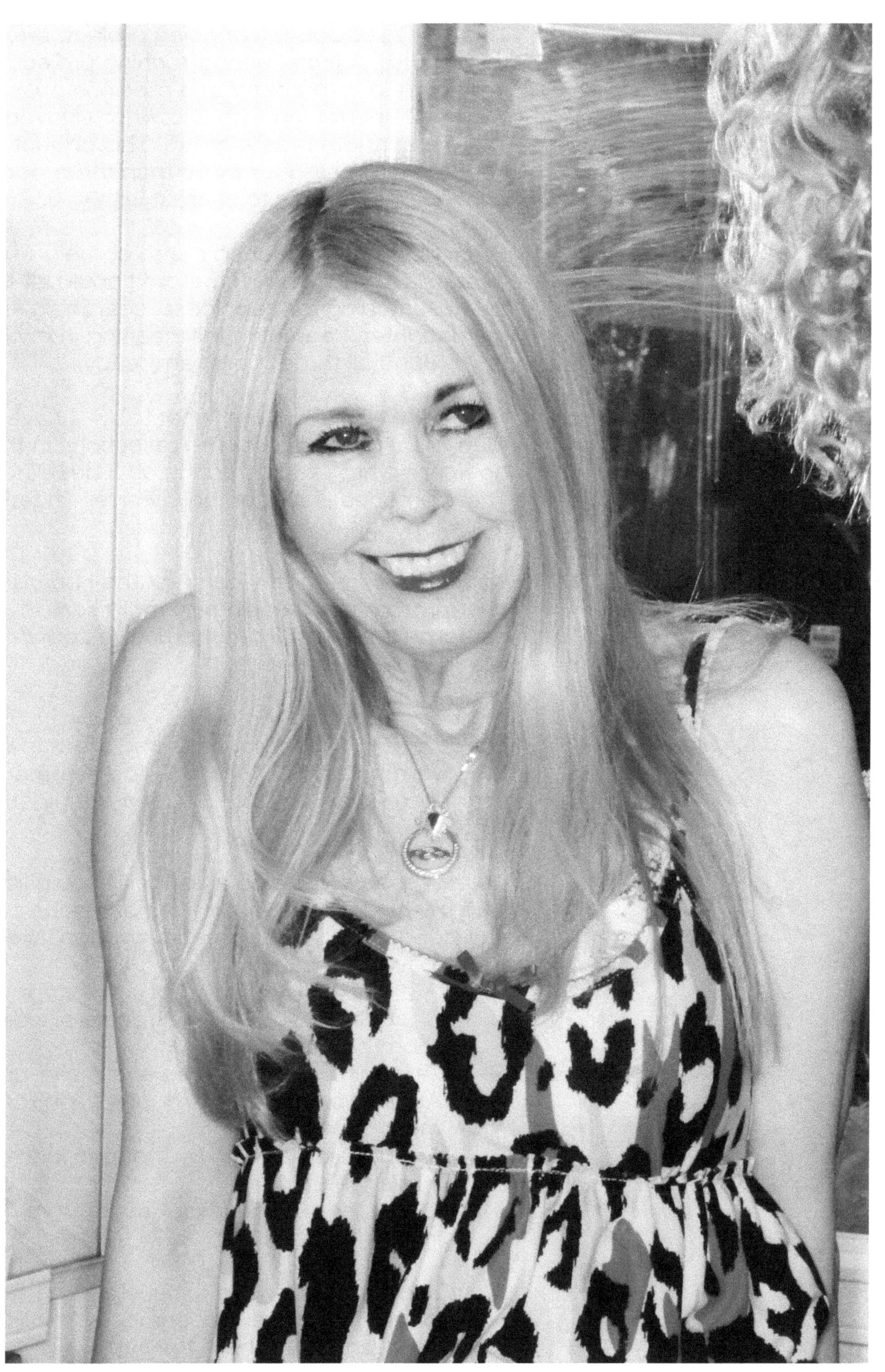

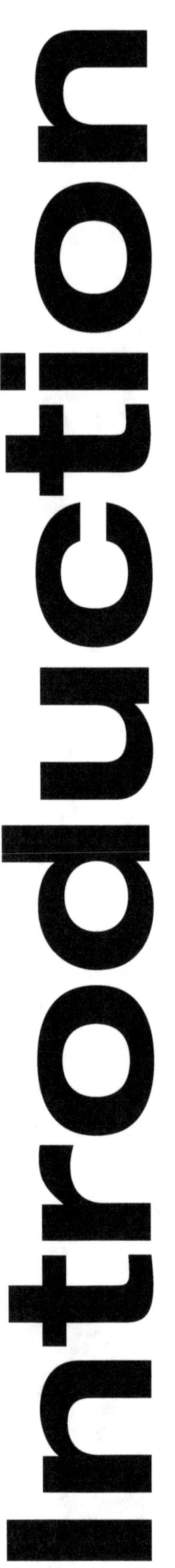

This is my project. My ongoing project, one of my private projects, a long-running project. A project filled with poetry and precious pussies. Women I spent time with and whom I loved. We loved one another as a group. This project has kept me interested for more than three decades and I am now ready to share it with you.

Backstage Girls needed me to come to stability in my own life before I could let it go. I was searching for happiness, searching for my daughter, searching for meaning in my life. I have found all three; now I am ready.

I hope the "Girls" will like what I say—I have tried to be very honest. The reflections in this book are what I went through as a headliner. The memories I have of the O'Farrell Theatre are sadness.

Dancers posed for my camera and I heard the chatter from the dressing room. I heard low esteem—they would put themselves down but would smile for my lens.

I was doing something useful—I was documenting a lifestyle. I assured them that they were beautiful. I was able to see past their scars and hurt. I promised to share their stories. I listened.

But because I was also a dancer, I could listen with my heart. Standing in front of the long, smudged mirror, putting on layer upon layer of paint, I overheard their gossip:

> Chatter about men, their dealers, kids, roommates.
> Talk about drugs, shoes and make-up.
> About working too hard, putting in too many hours.
> About being pawed by the men in the audience.
> About the soreness that came from deep in their souls...

Most had given up, were exhausted and accepting of their fate. But some...some like me still had dreams. And here they are.

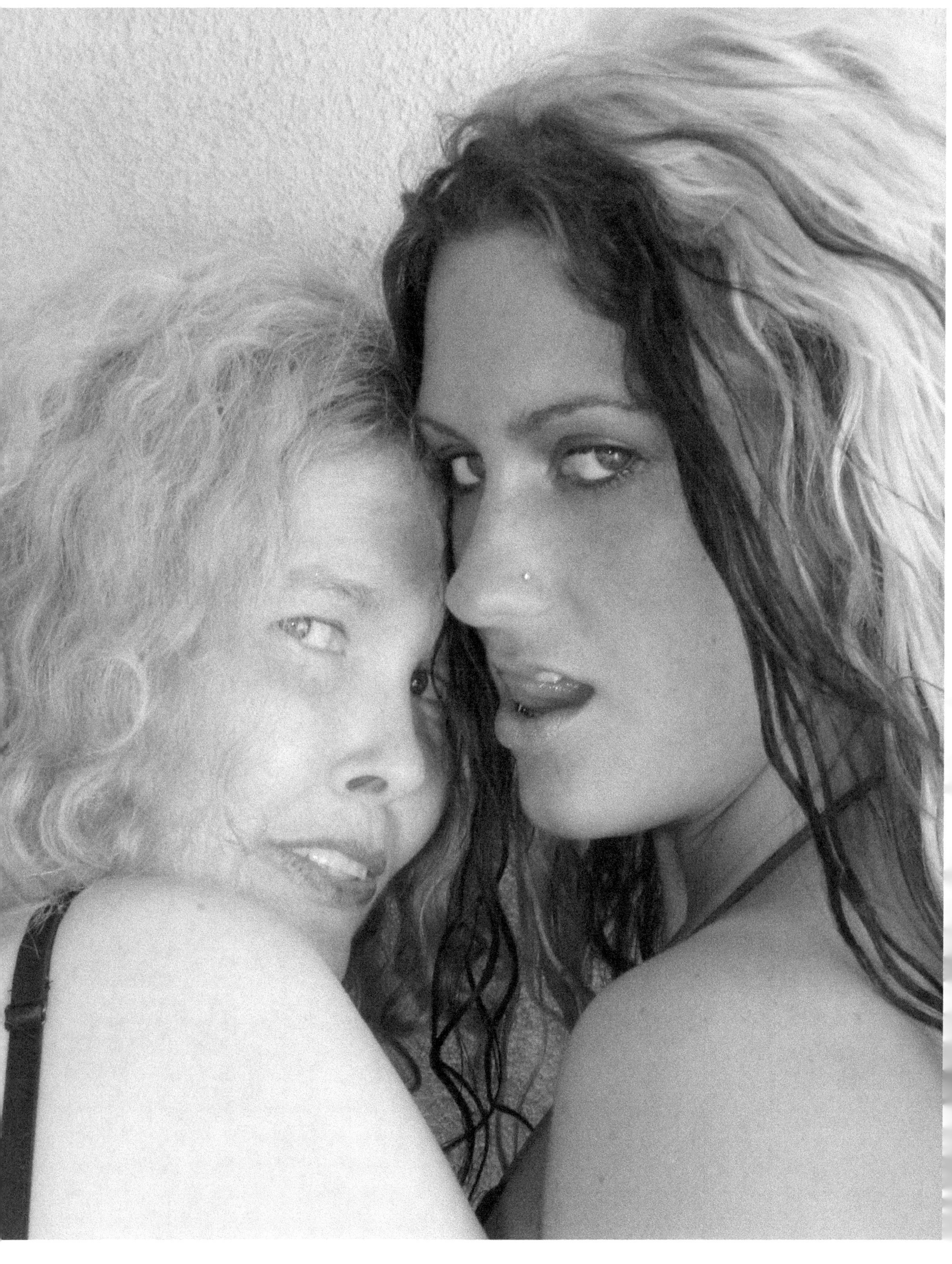

Before...

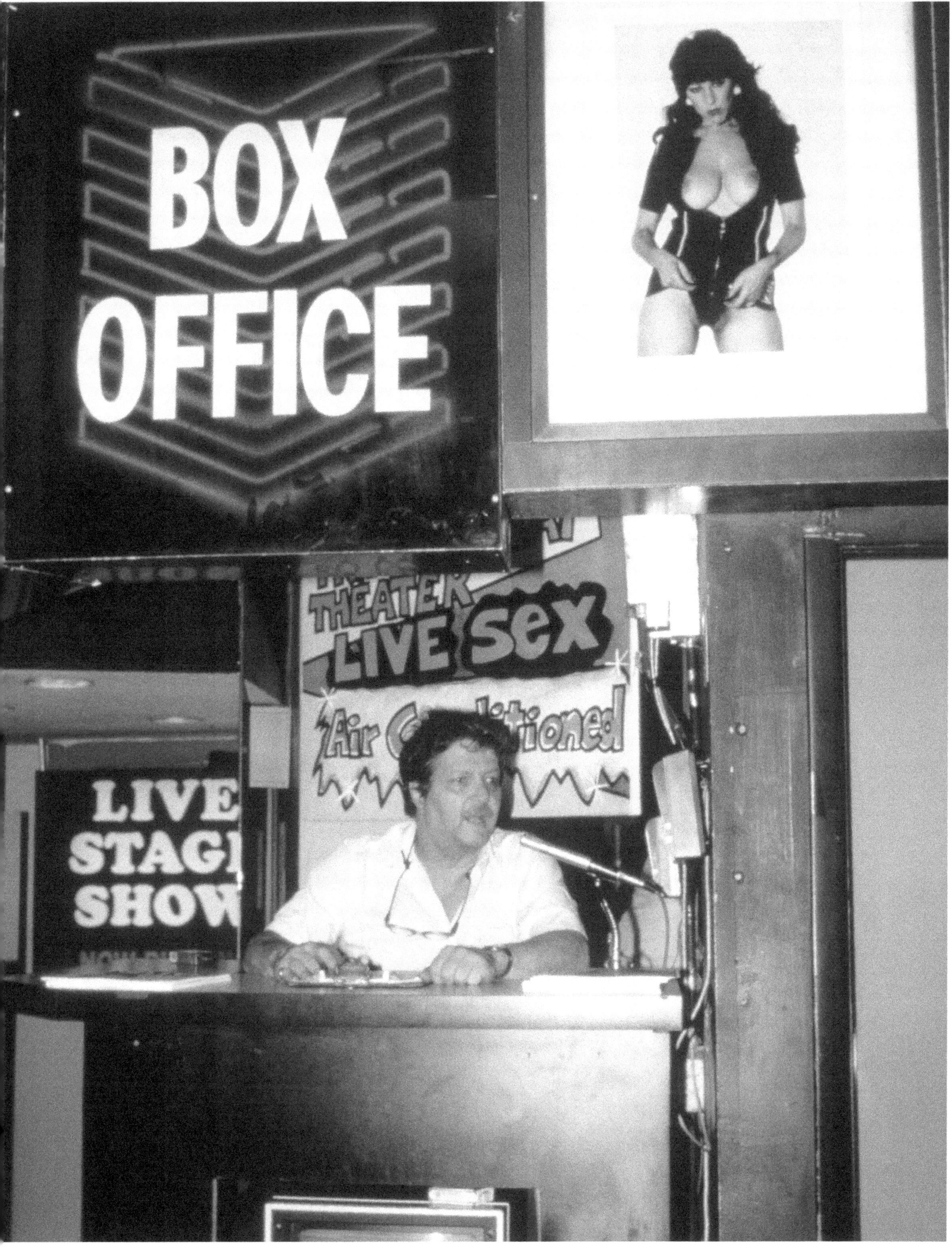
BOX
OFFICE
THEATER
LIVE sex
Air

Therapist

When anyone asks
what I do,
I say
I'm a therapist,
that I'm an artist.

But in reality,
I nurse lonely, old men.
I'm a dancer.

I always lie.

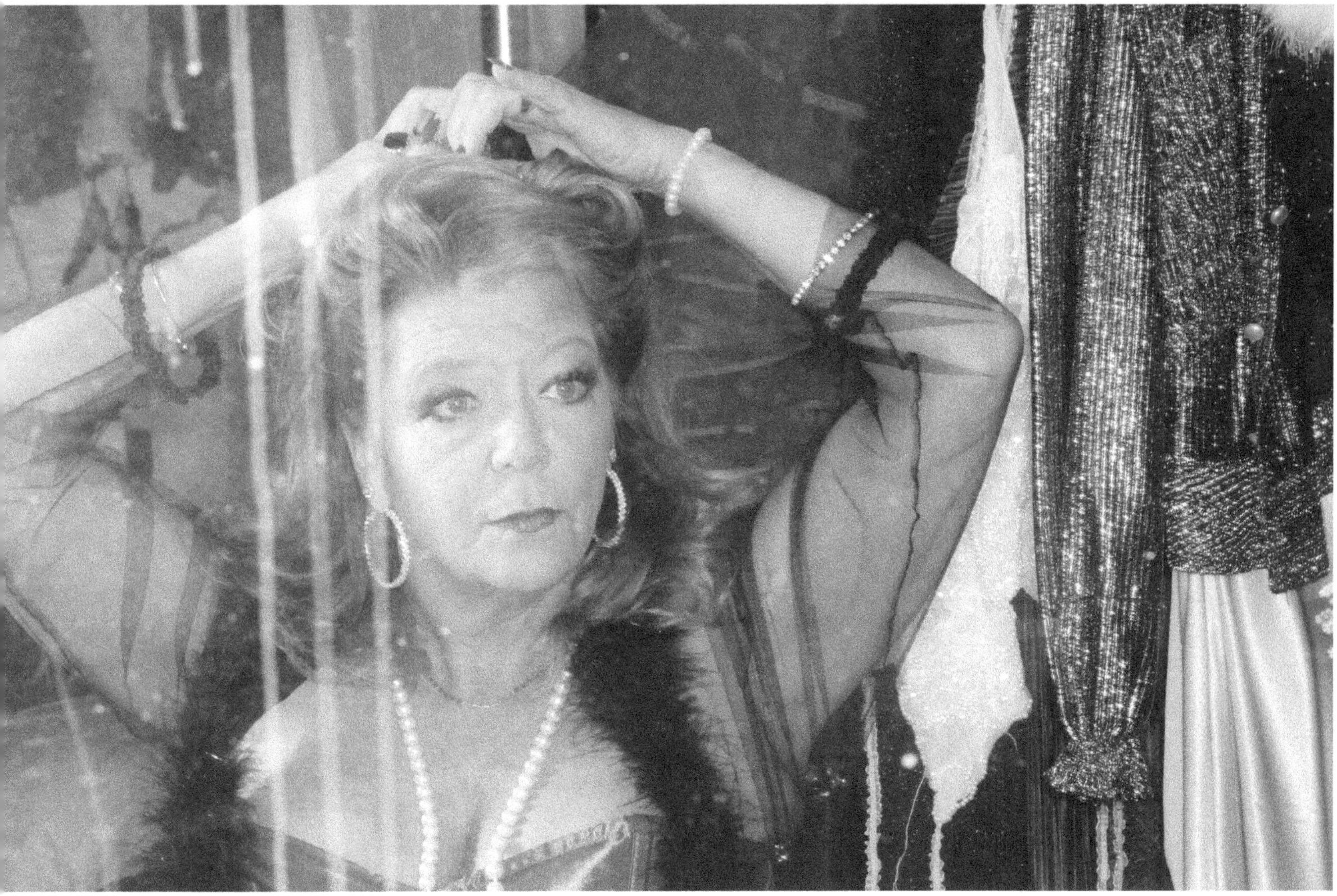

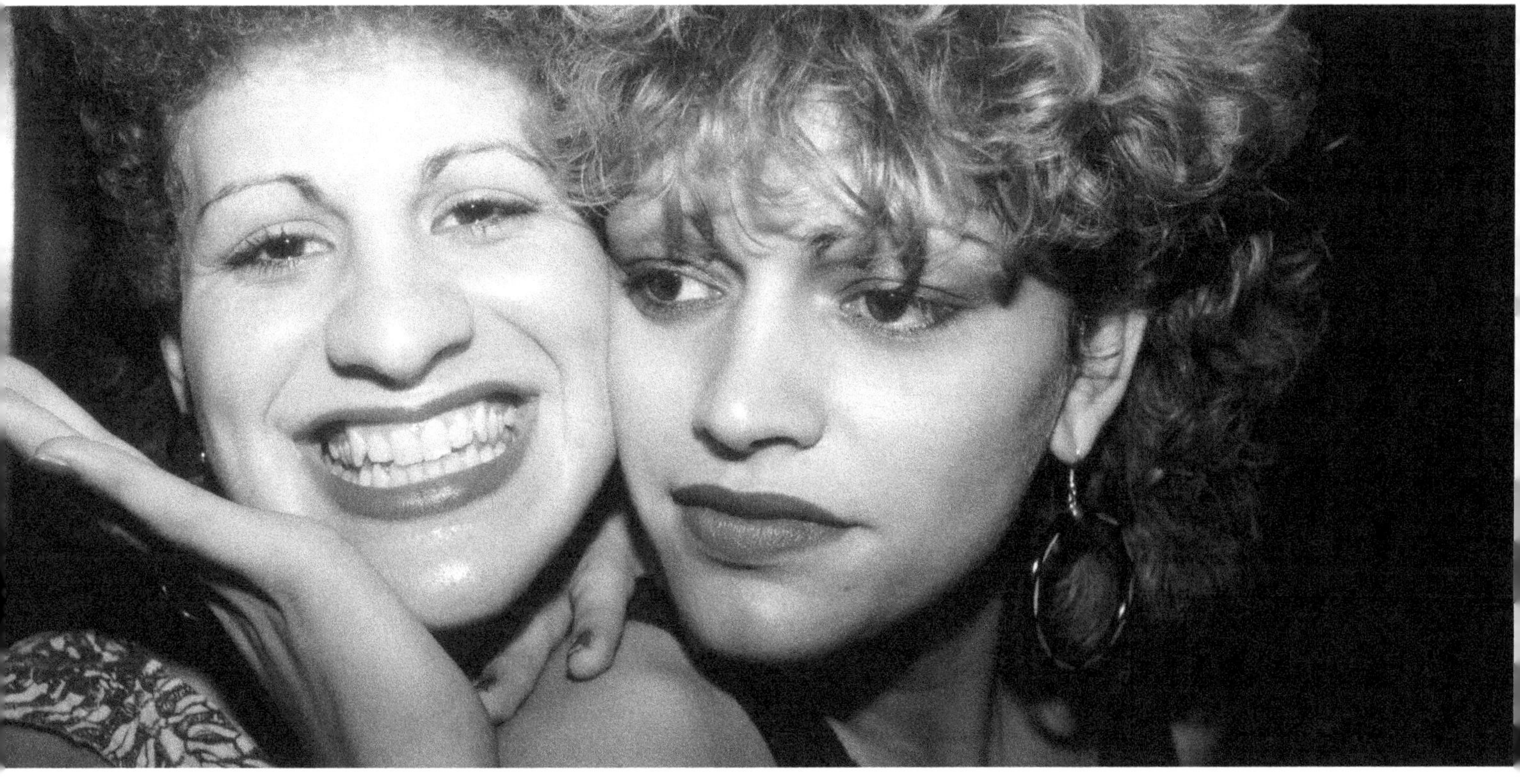

Call Me Human

We have been called:
broads,
dogs,
chicks,
tomatoes,
dames,
foxes,
bitches,
cows,
pigs,
whores
and
cunts.

We are humans.

Potions

Lotions,
sprays,
oils,
mists,
roll-ons...
pussy potions.

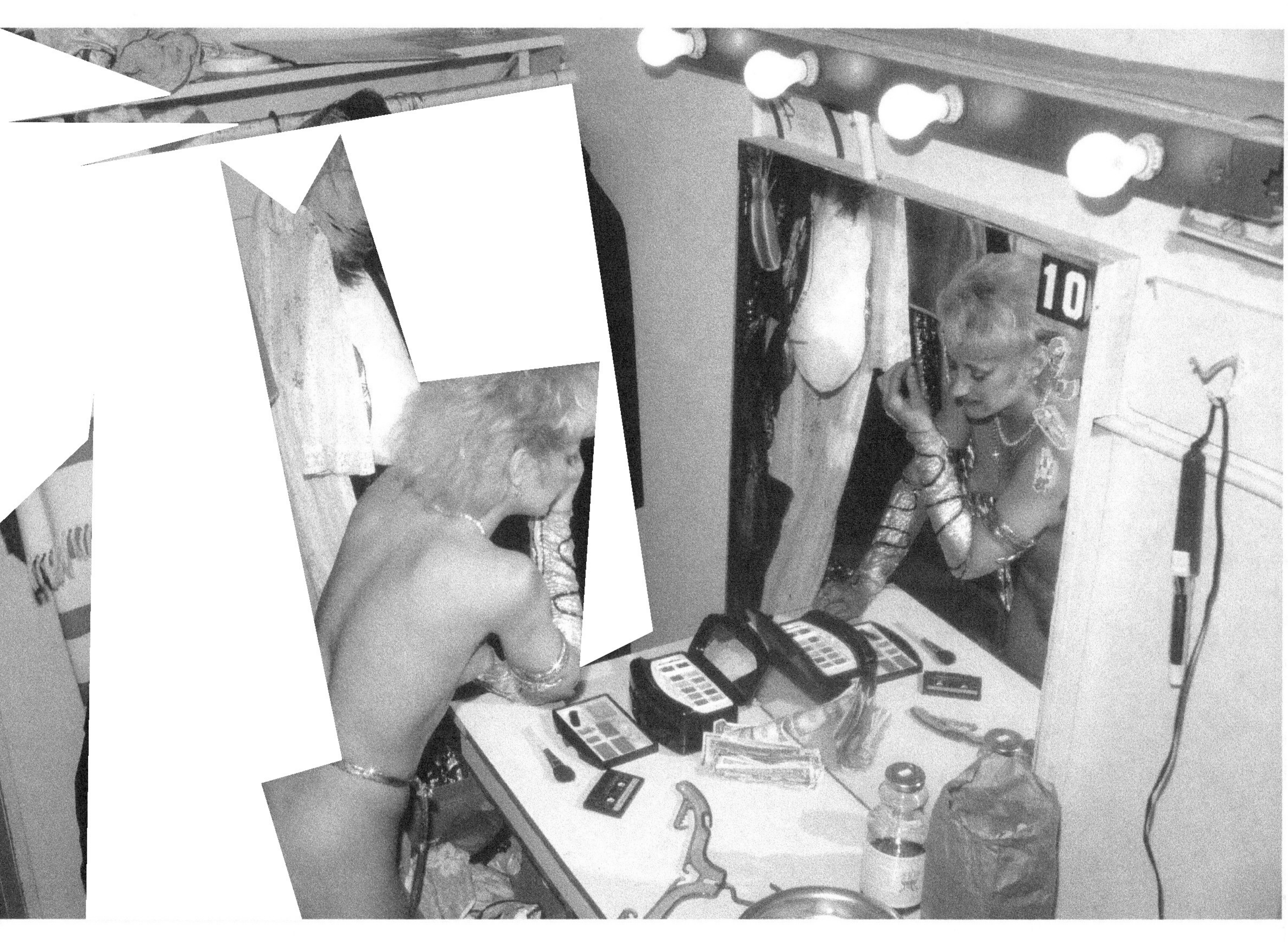
10

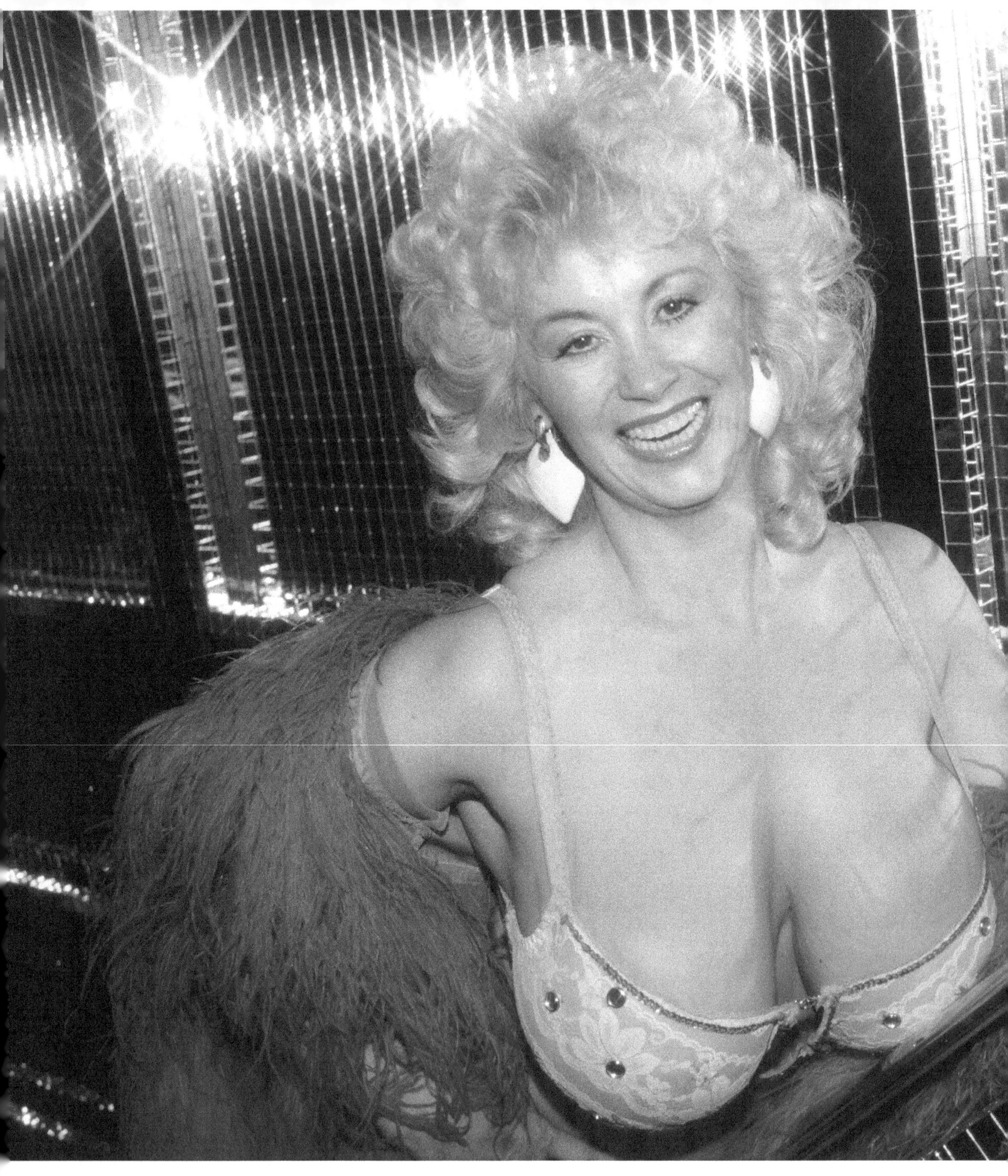

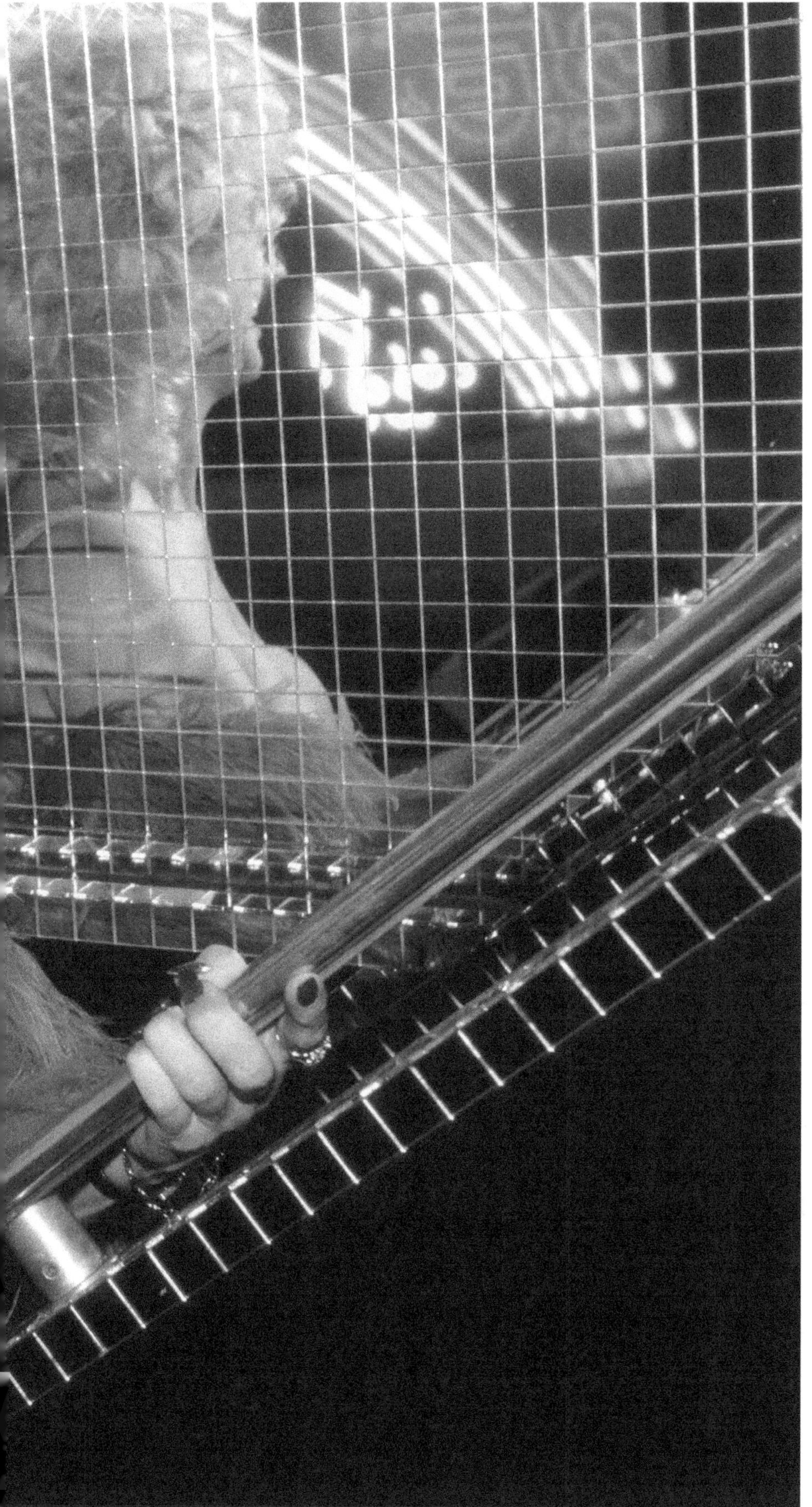

Pretty Pain

Pretty pain,
putting you on.
Putting on a face
of prettiness.

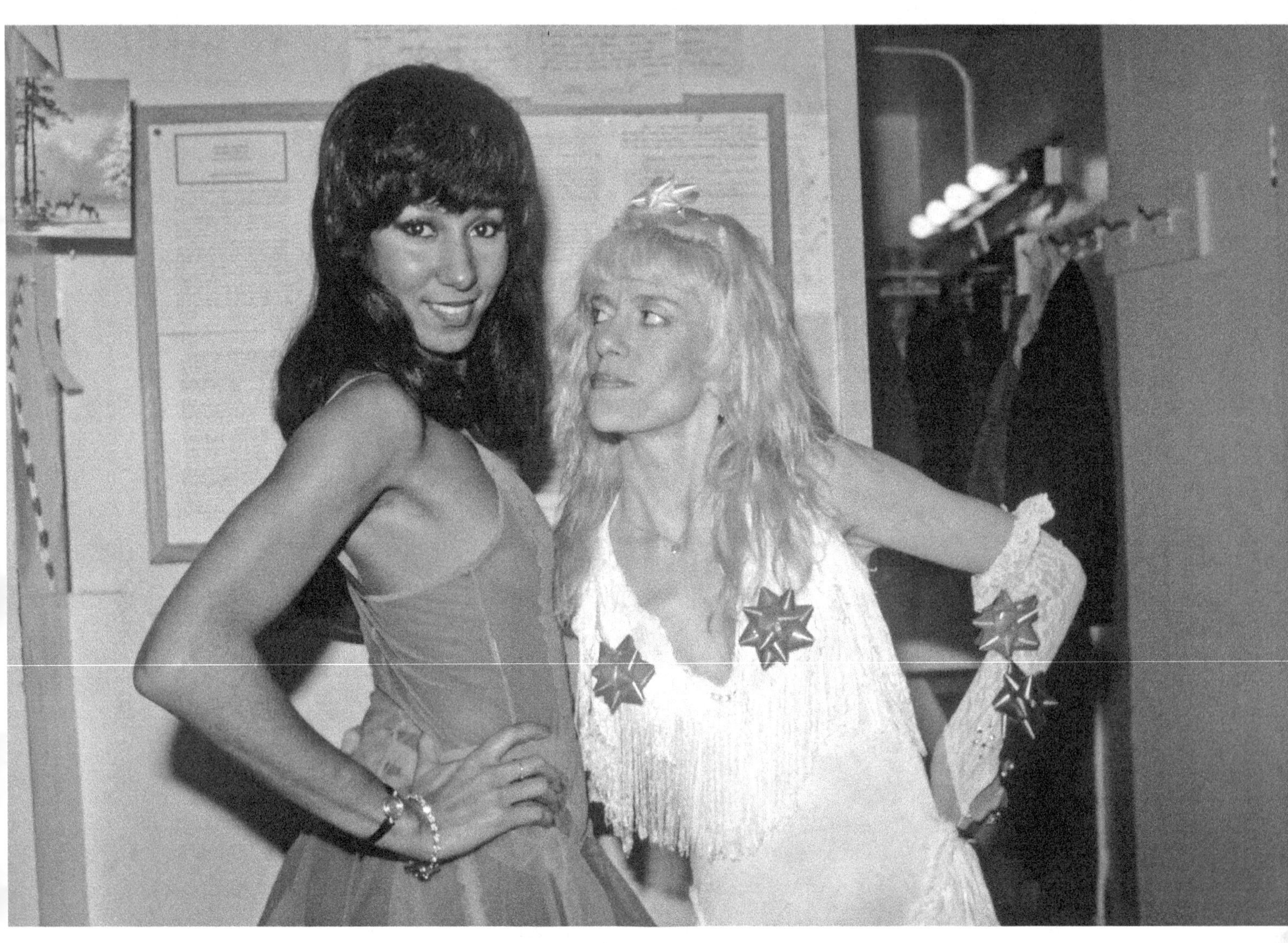

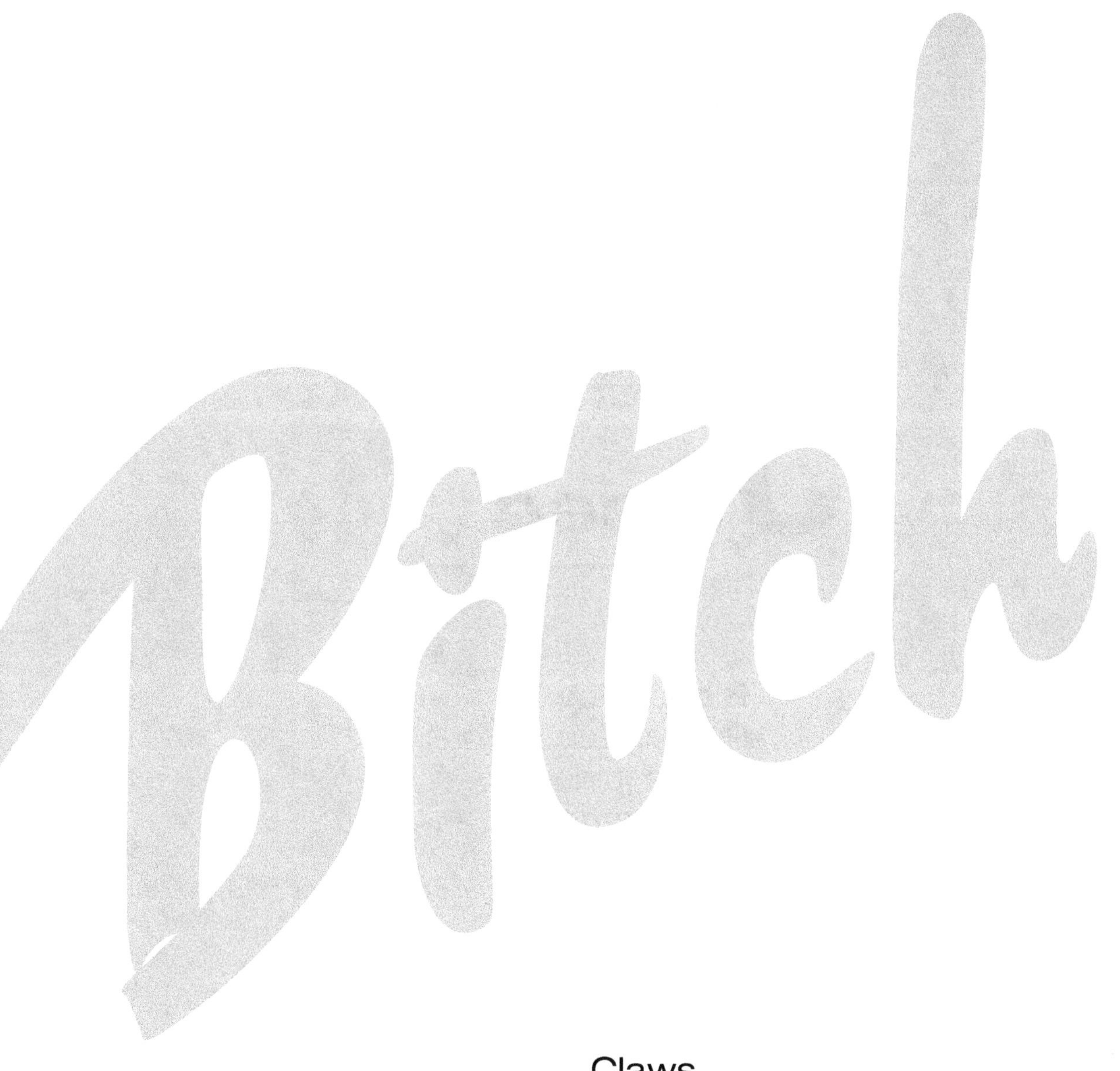

Claws
Shy
Animal
Coy
Passion
Wink
Cat-eyes
Sickly
Sweet

Bitch

Juiced

Blood juice.
Pussy juice.
Grape juice,
Fermented.
Blacks.
Whites.
Jews.
Putting on
and
taking off
their clothes
all day long.

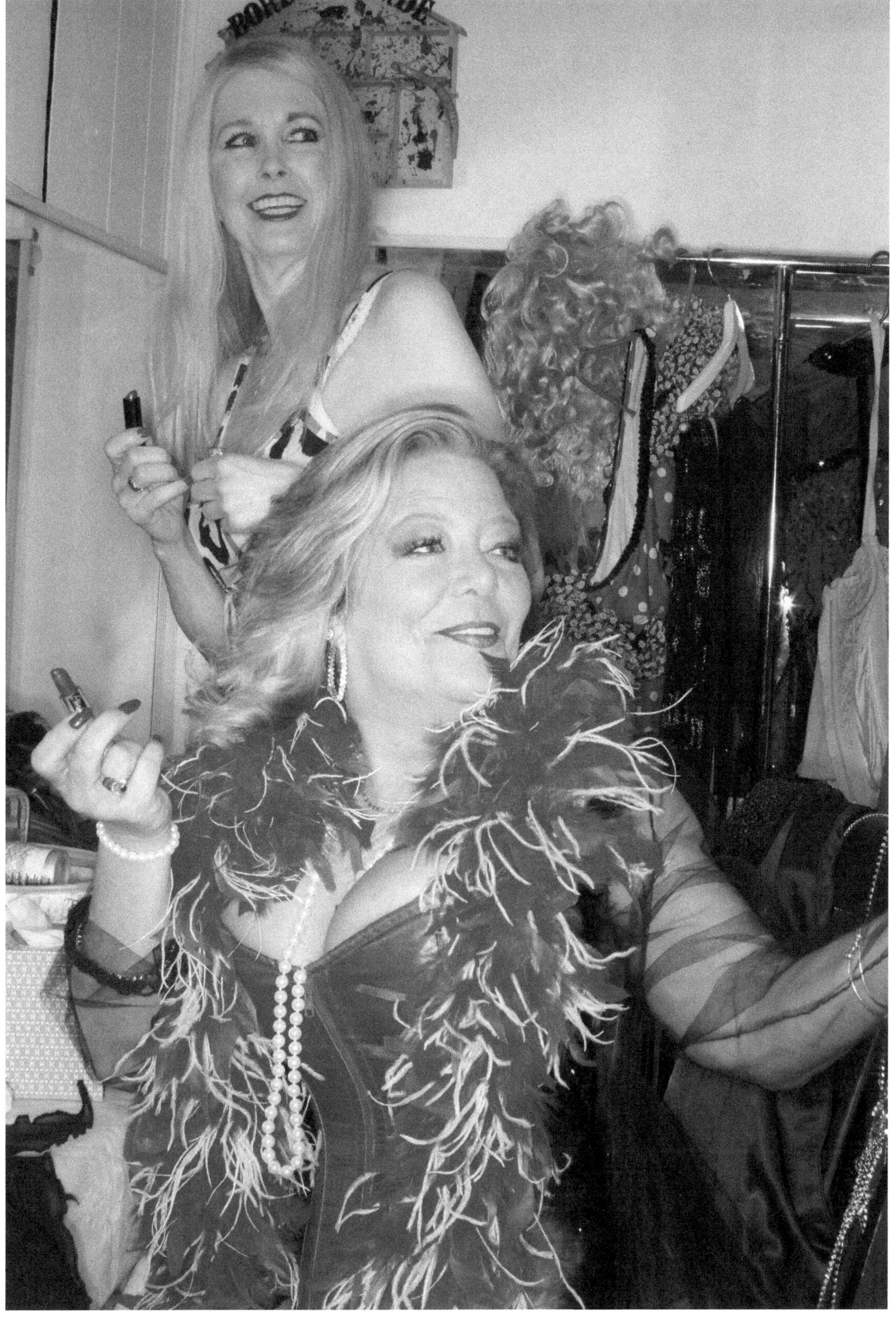

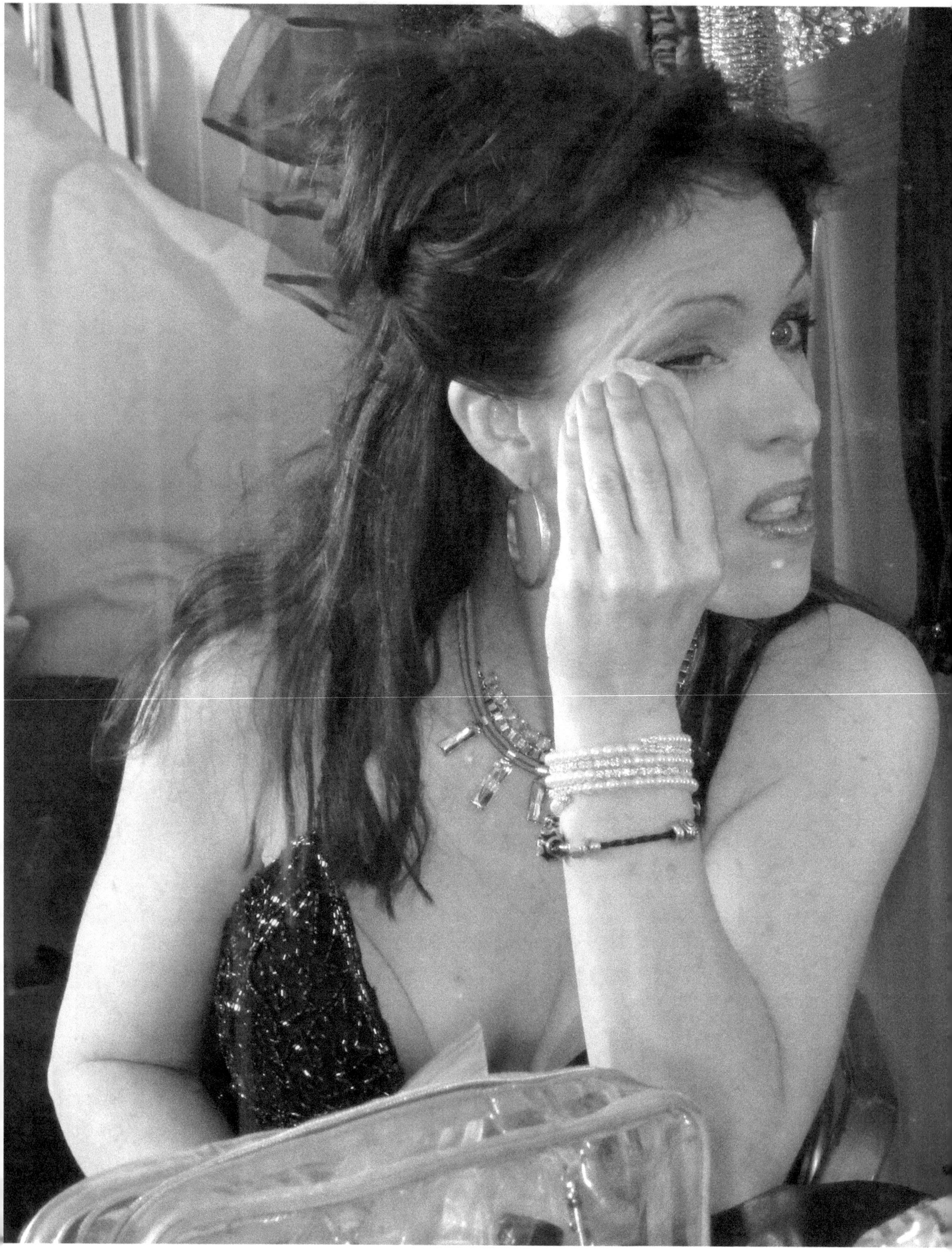

Making Up

Put on more.
Heavier lips.
Always as
red as red.
Darker eyeshadow,
whiter masque.
Hide behind
false eyelashes.
Throw red kisses.

Hanging Out

Shaved cunts,
bodies stretch-marked.

Locker room
full of perfume,
lights galore.

Someone squeals,
screams.
Another laughs.

Countertops dusty,
waste can overflowing.

Will you zip me up?

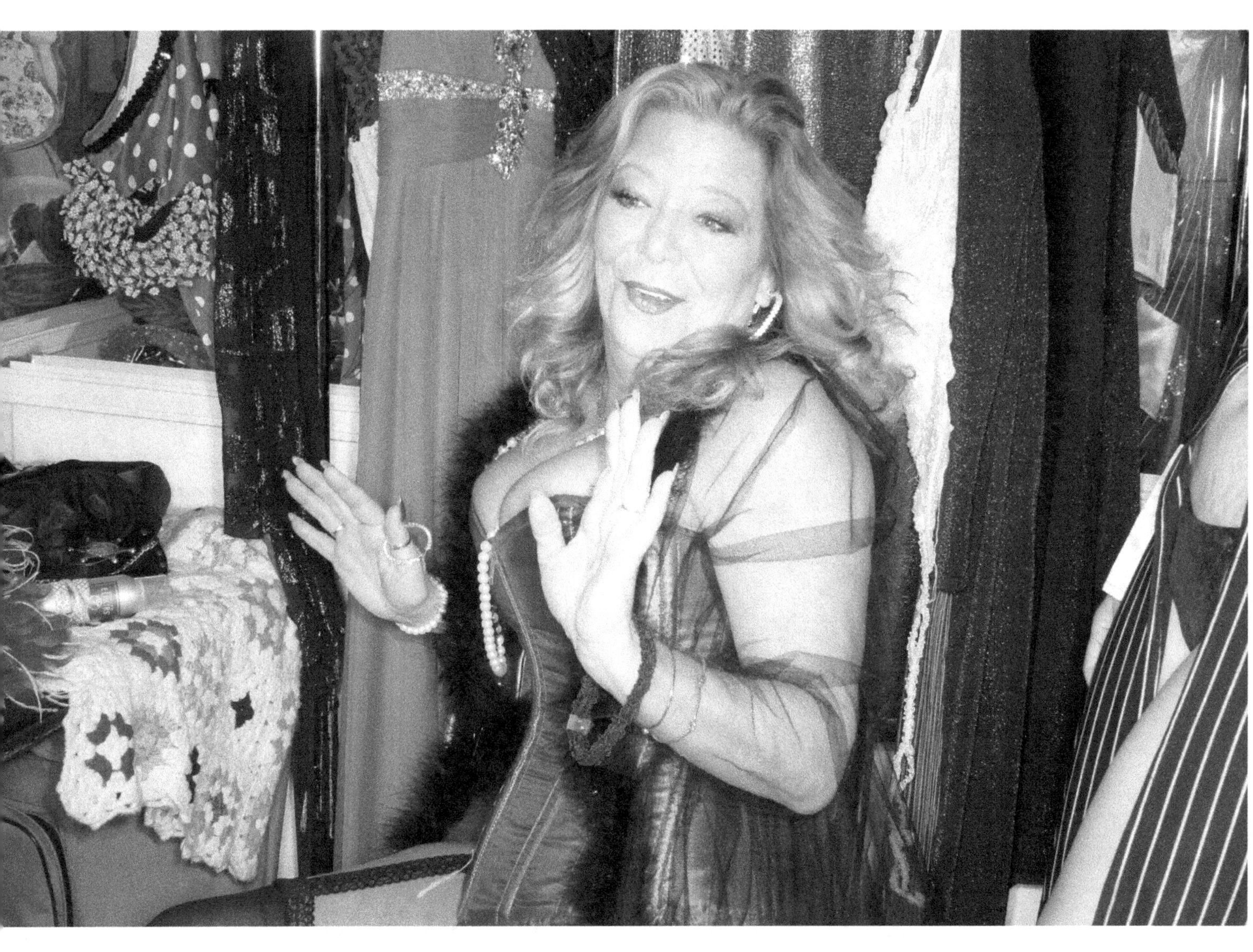

Five Minutes!

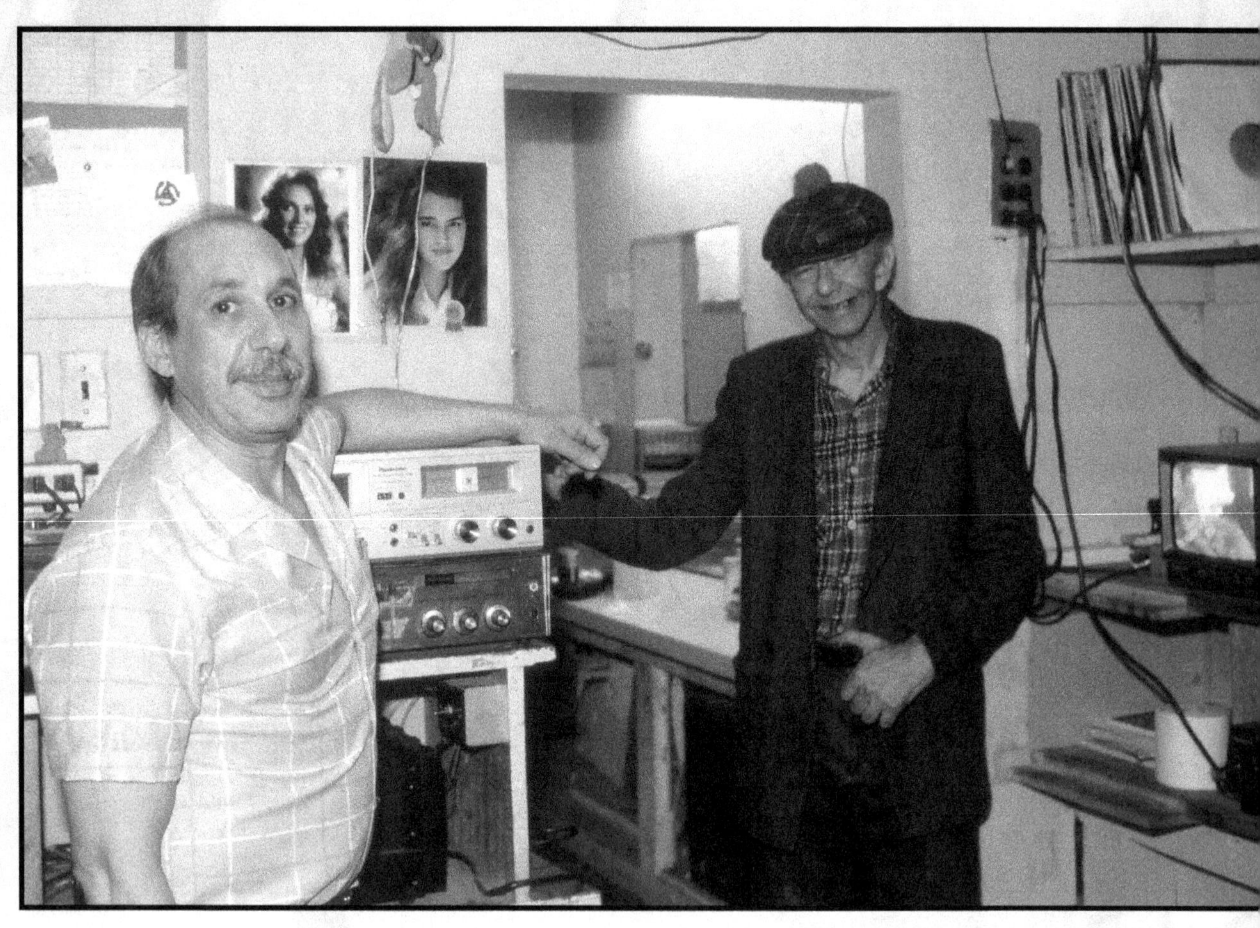

Get ready, girls,
five minutes!

Always five.
Act alive—
the Daddies
are out there.

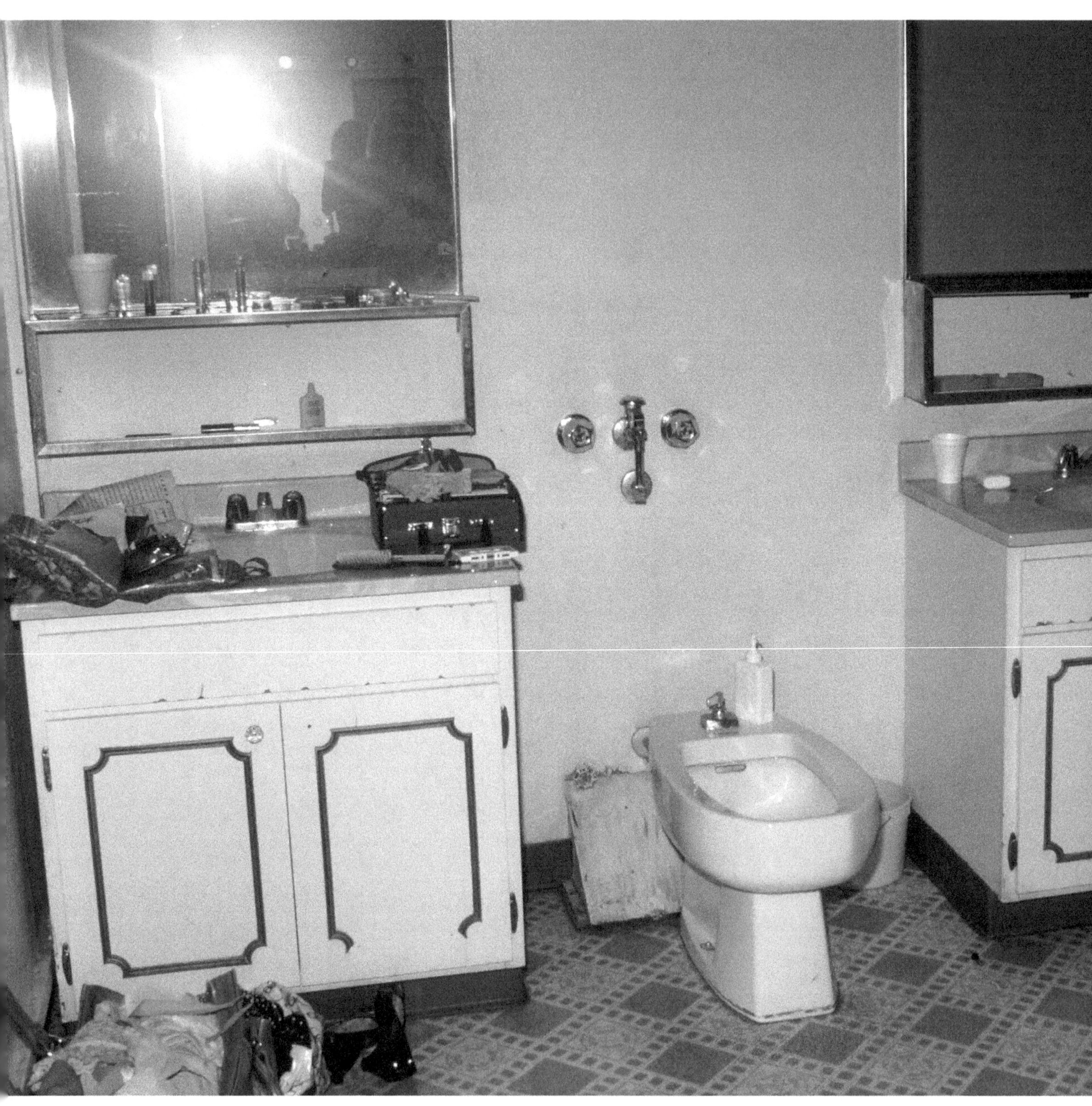

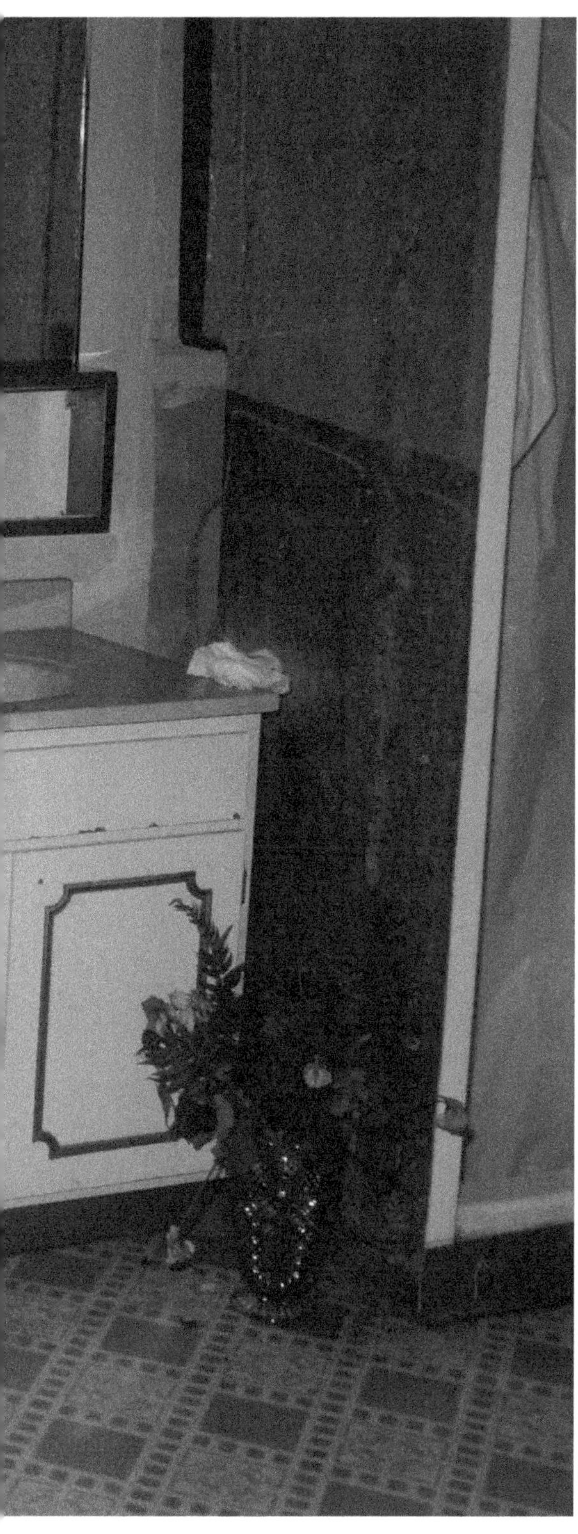

The Ward

There is no reward.

This is, for most,
a ward of disease.

Slaves
of sexual liberation,
trapped.

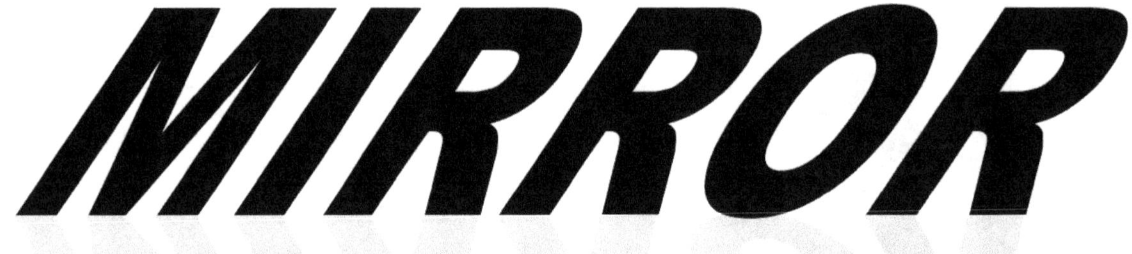

Applied faces
talk to each other
only
through the mirror glass.

Smoke pours out
from lipstick lips
thick with crimson.

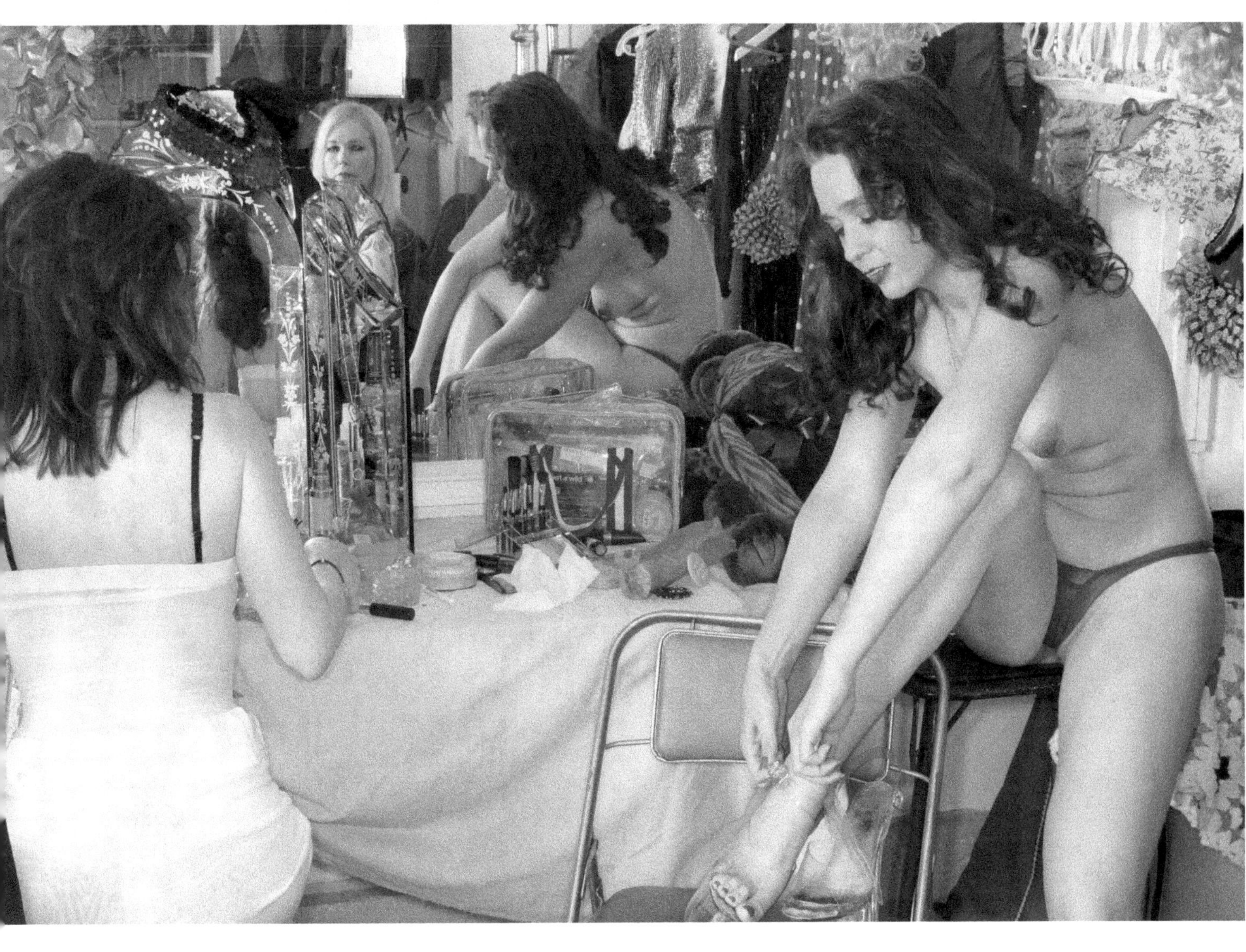

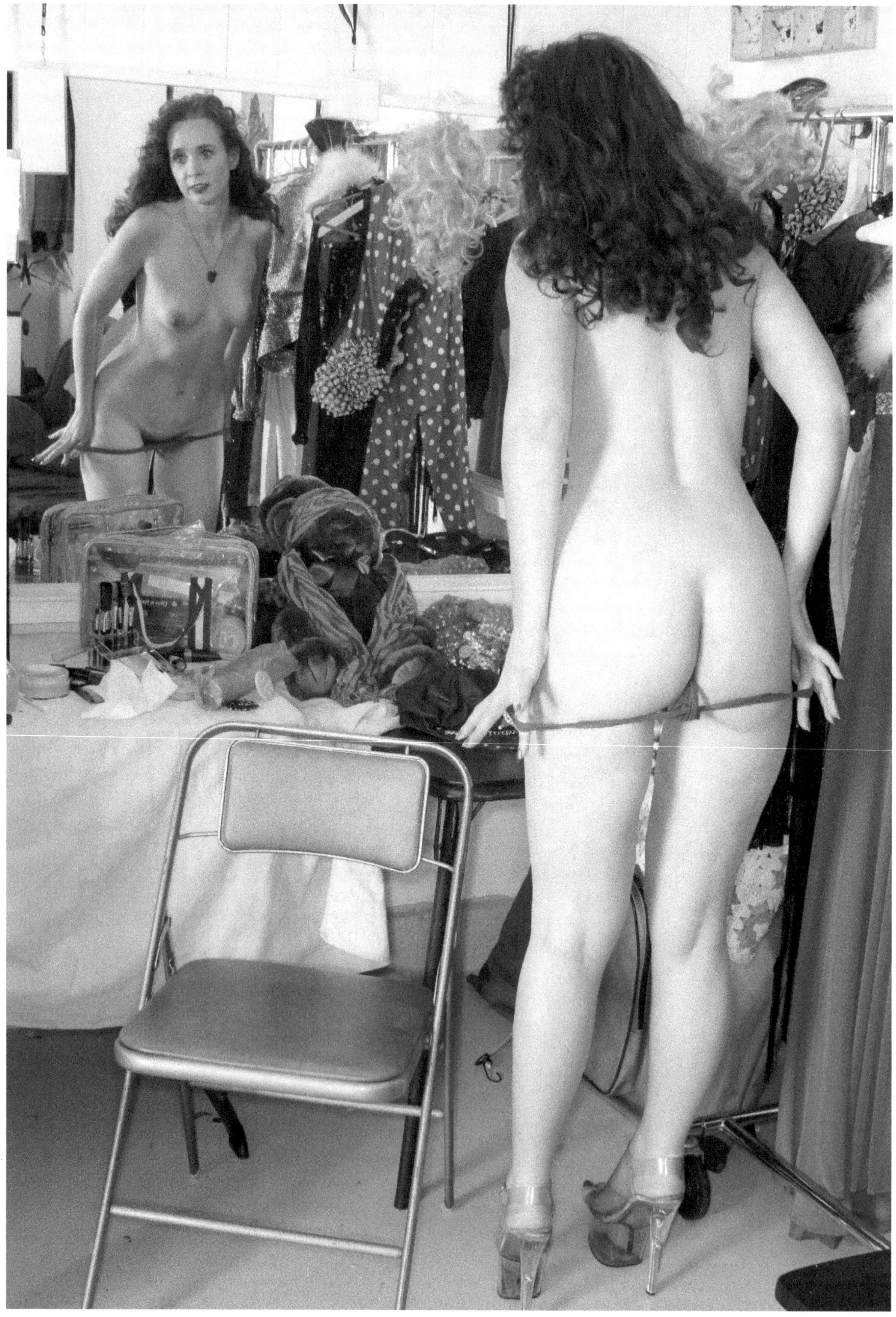

Guilt

I urge them
to shower,
to wash away
their guilt.

The boss man
runs in
and yells,
"Hurry up!"

They do,
and exit in a fog
of perfume,
still stale.

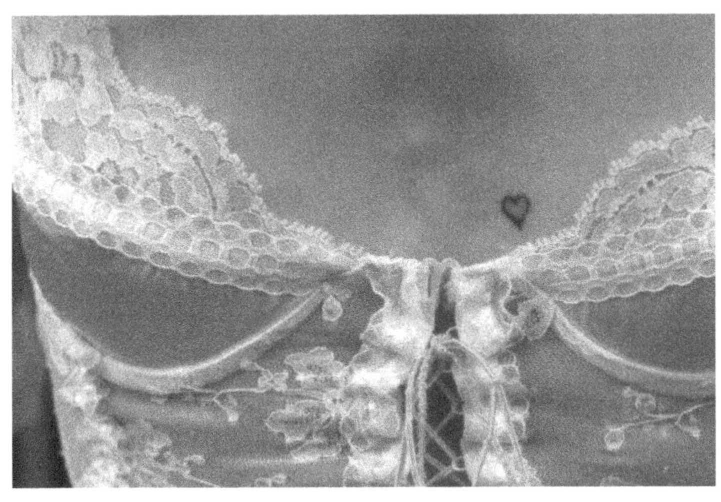

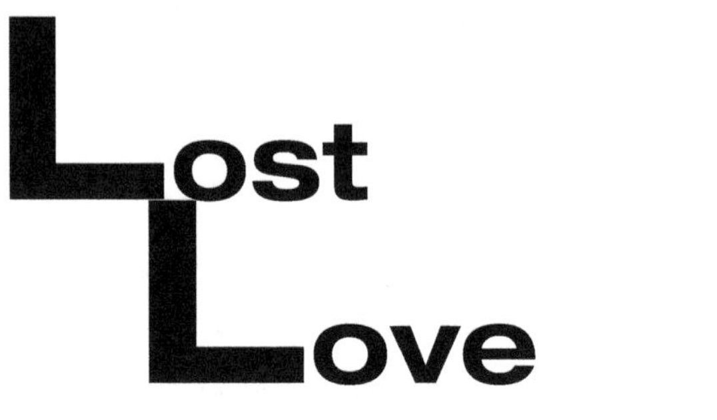

Lost Love

Show off.

Heat up your blood.
Track marks on your arms.
Dead skin on your legs.
Lost love in your memory.

Do a hot show!

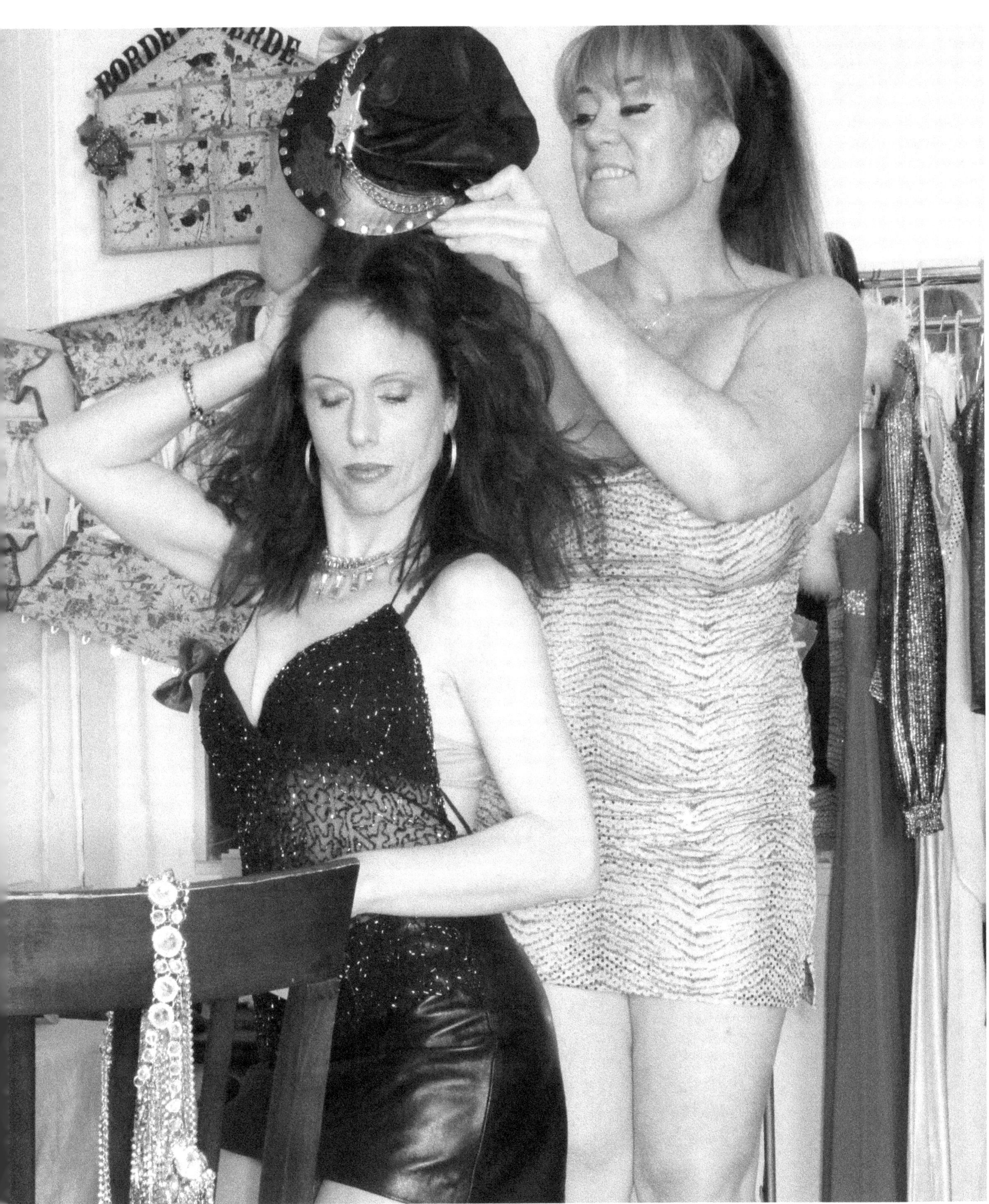

During...

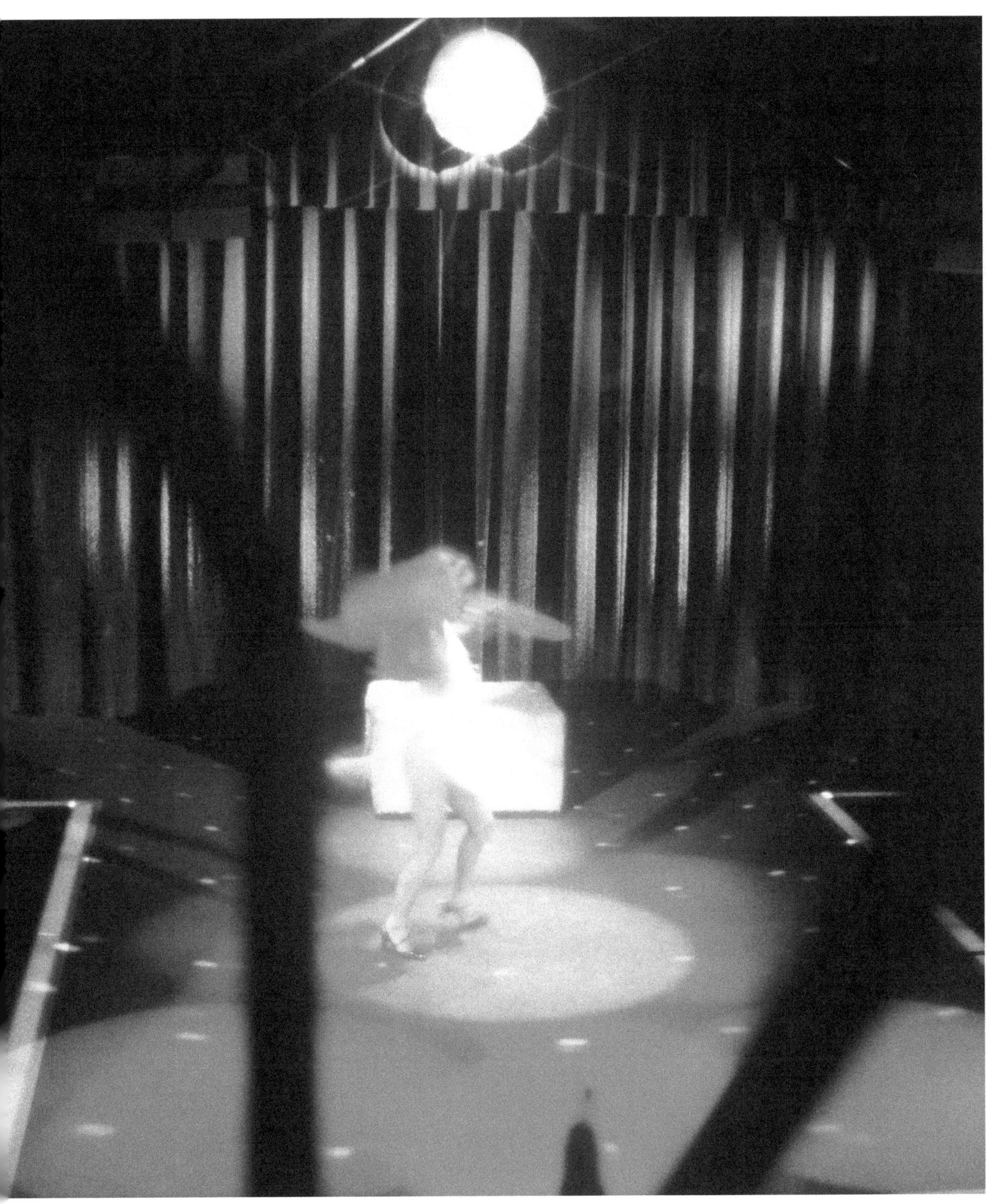

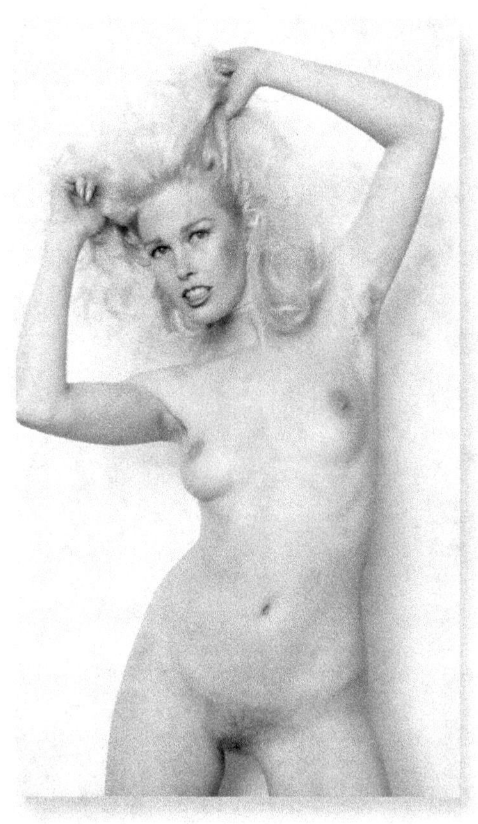

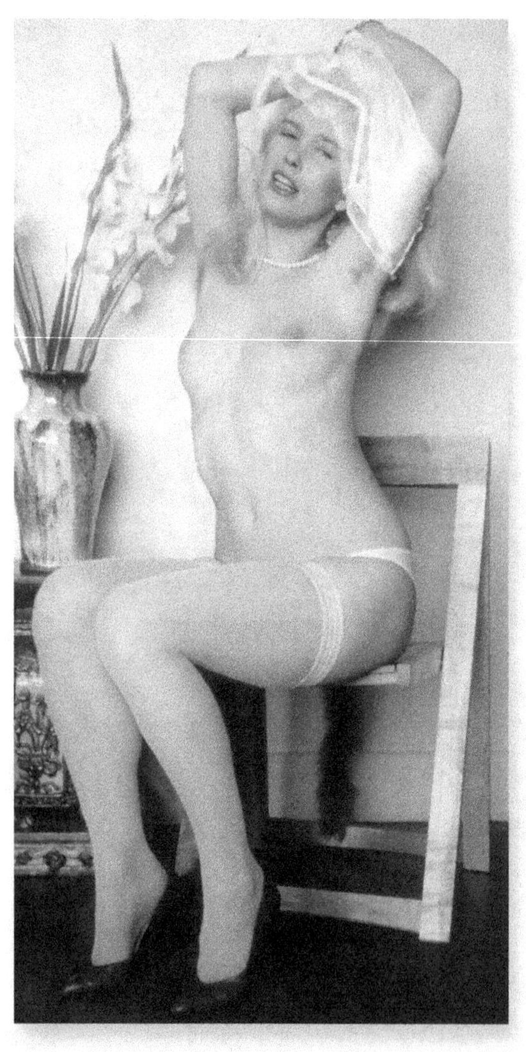

Showgirls

This is what a girl looks like.

(I am invulnerable
because I am
somewhere else.)

Take off the blouse
on the first song,
get naked
by the third.

Drowning in Notes

Go on.
Onstage.
Loud music.
Louder, please.
Drown my thoughts
in your notes.

Drums beat my ears
and I strip.

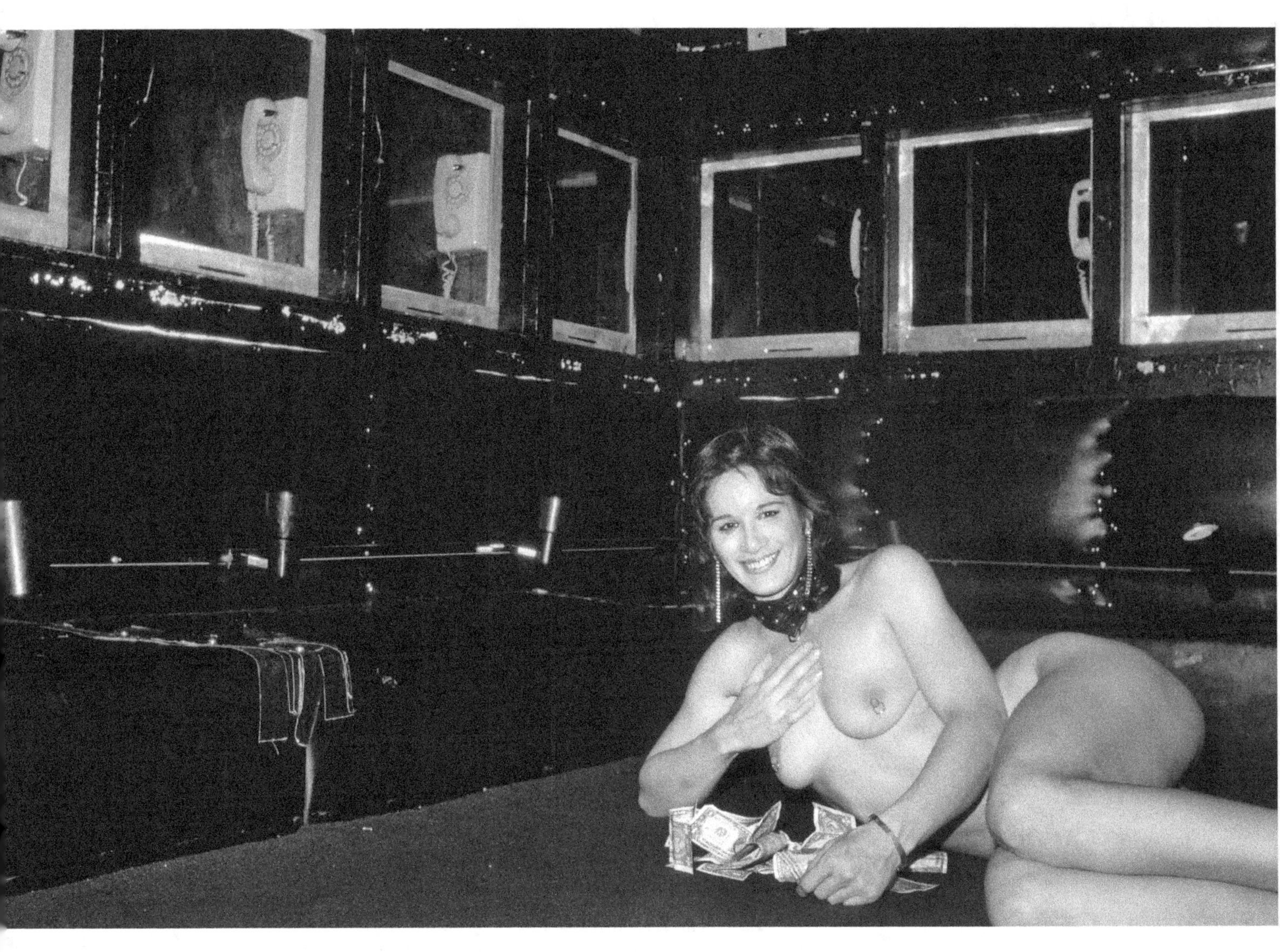

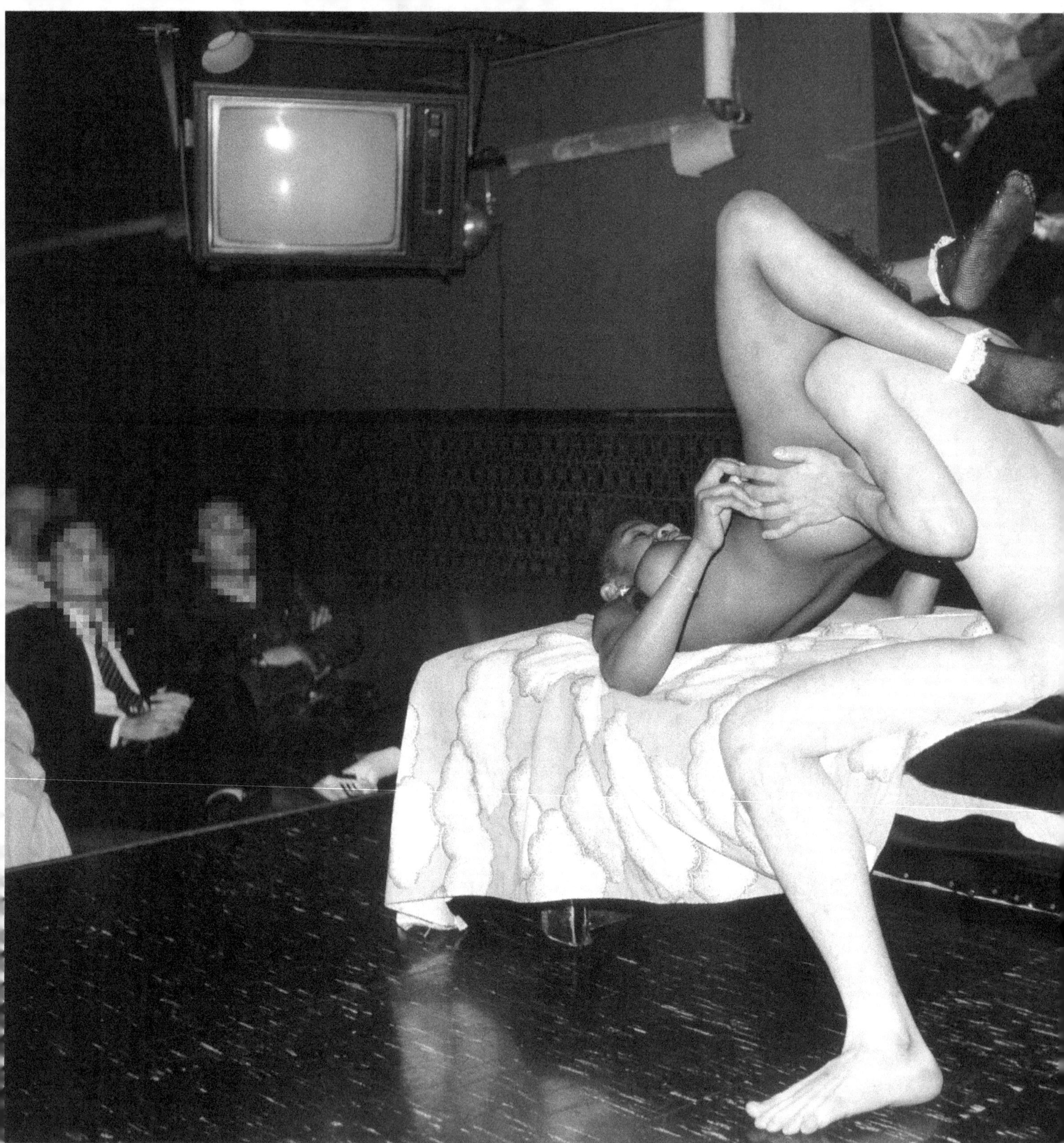

Tour Busses

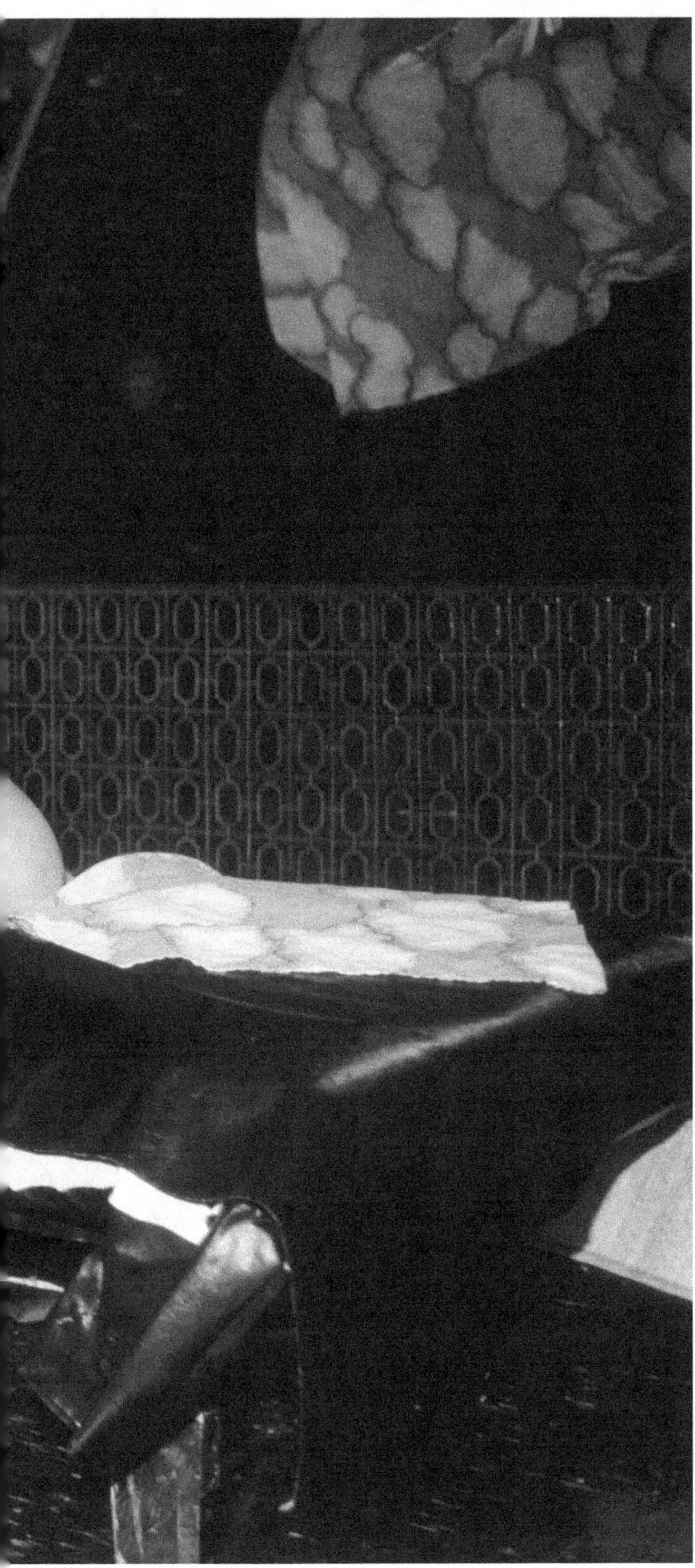

Tour busses
line up
in the bus zone,
deposit
little Japanese men
to stare at us.

Sanity

How to talk yourself
into sanity
while laying
on your bare ass,
pulling apart your pussy lips.

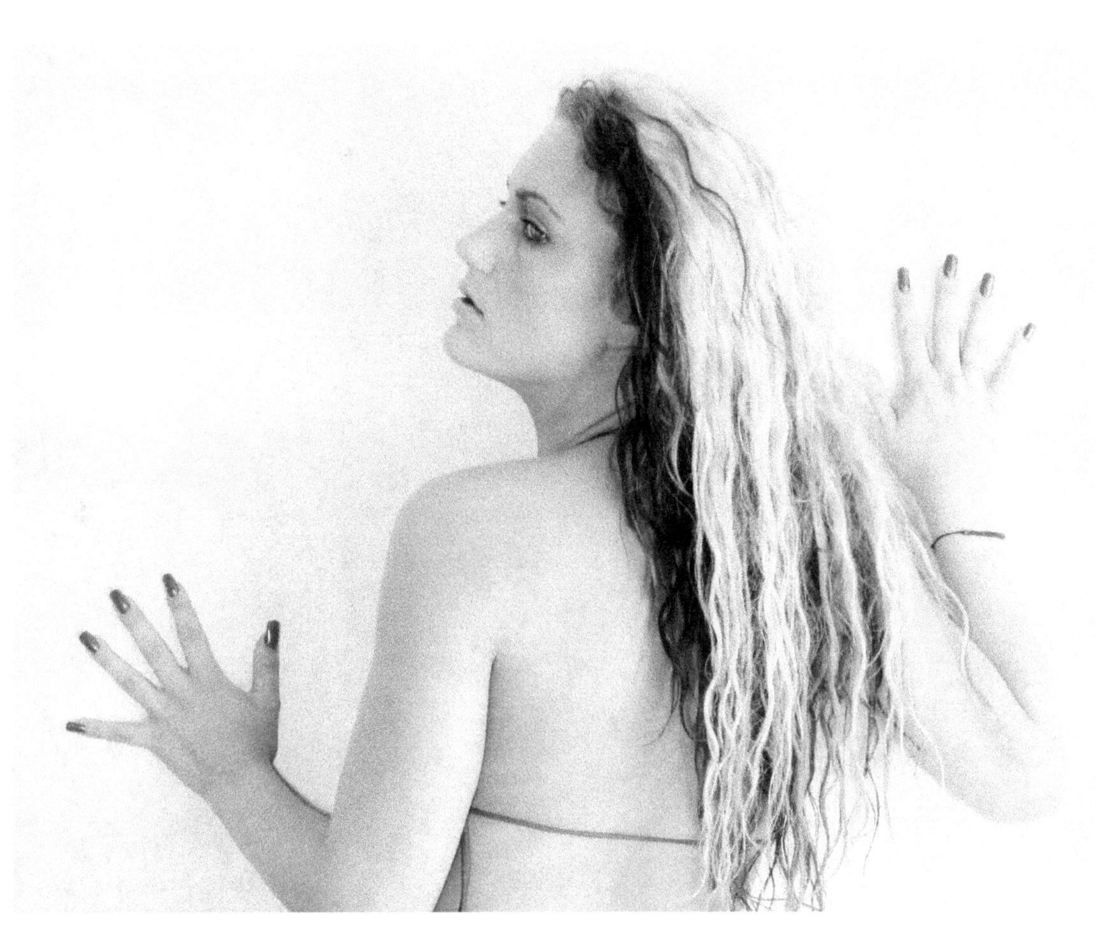

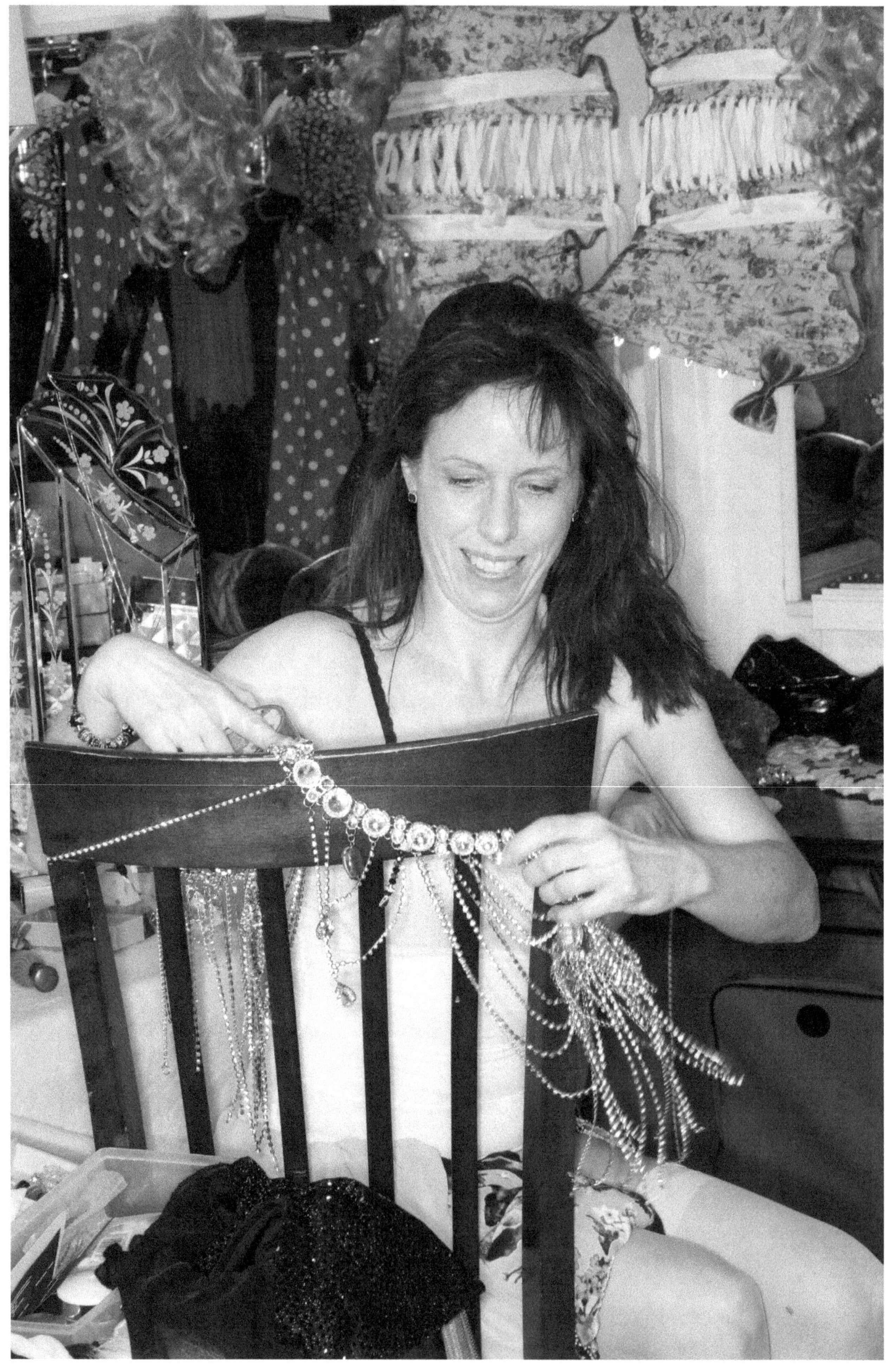

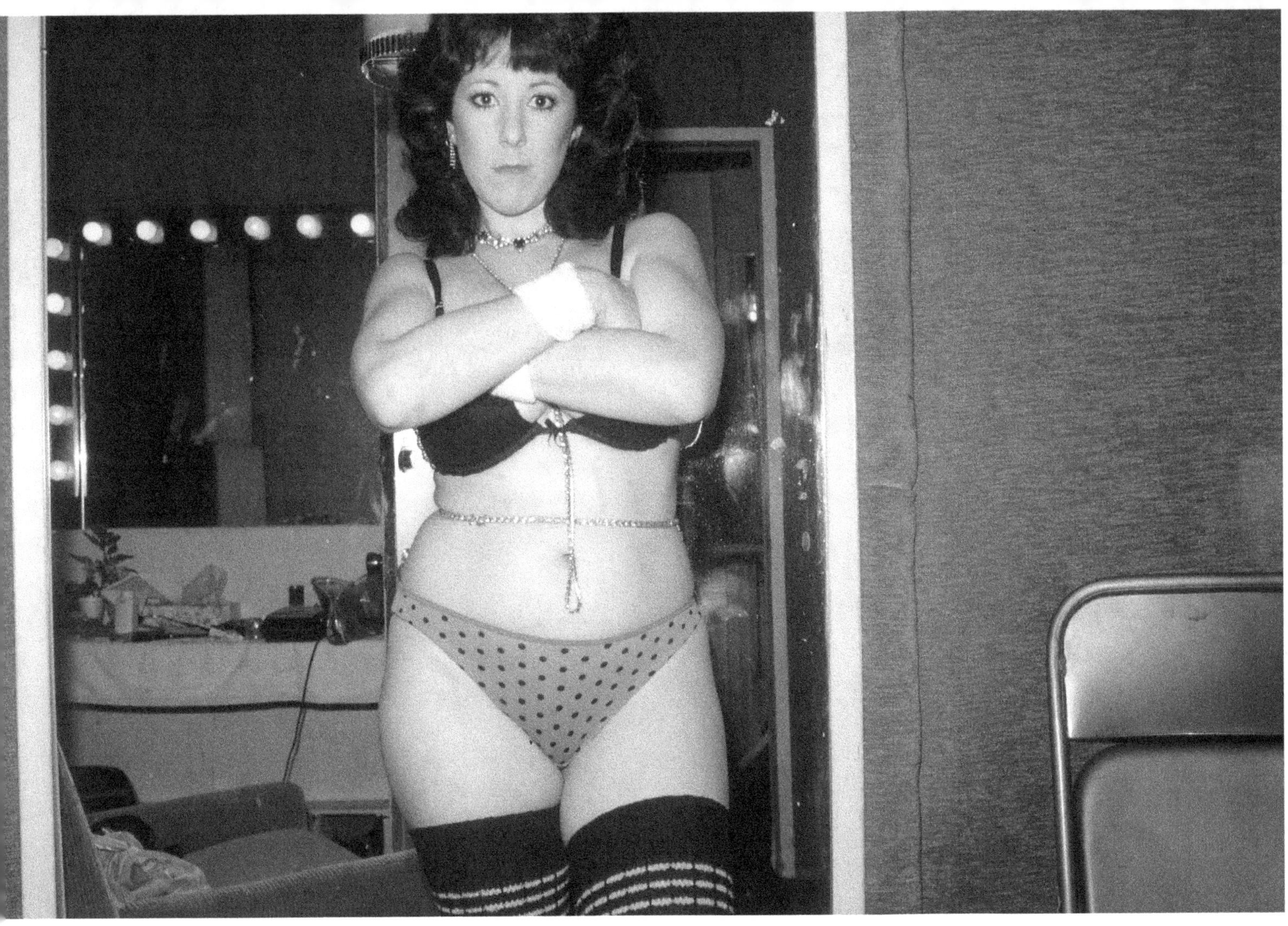

Yours

Vixen.
Amazon.
Vamp.
Trash.
Lady.
Whore.
Soul.
Ego.

Yours
for the taking.

San Francisco's Tenderloin District

Tender loins.
Tenderloin.
Tenderloin tails.
Legal tender.
Tender temptress.

Tend her.
Ten dollar.
Tale.

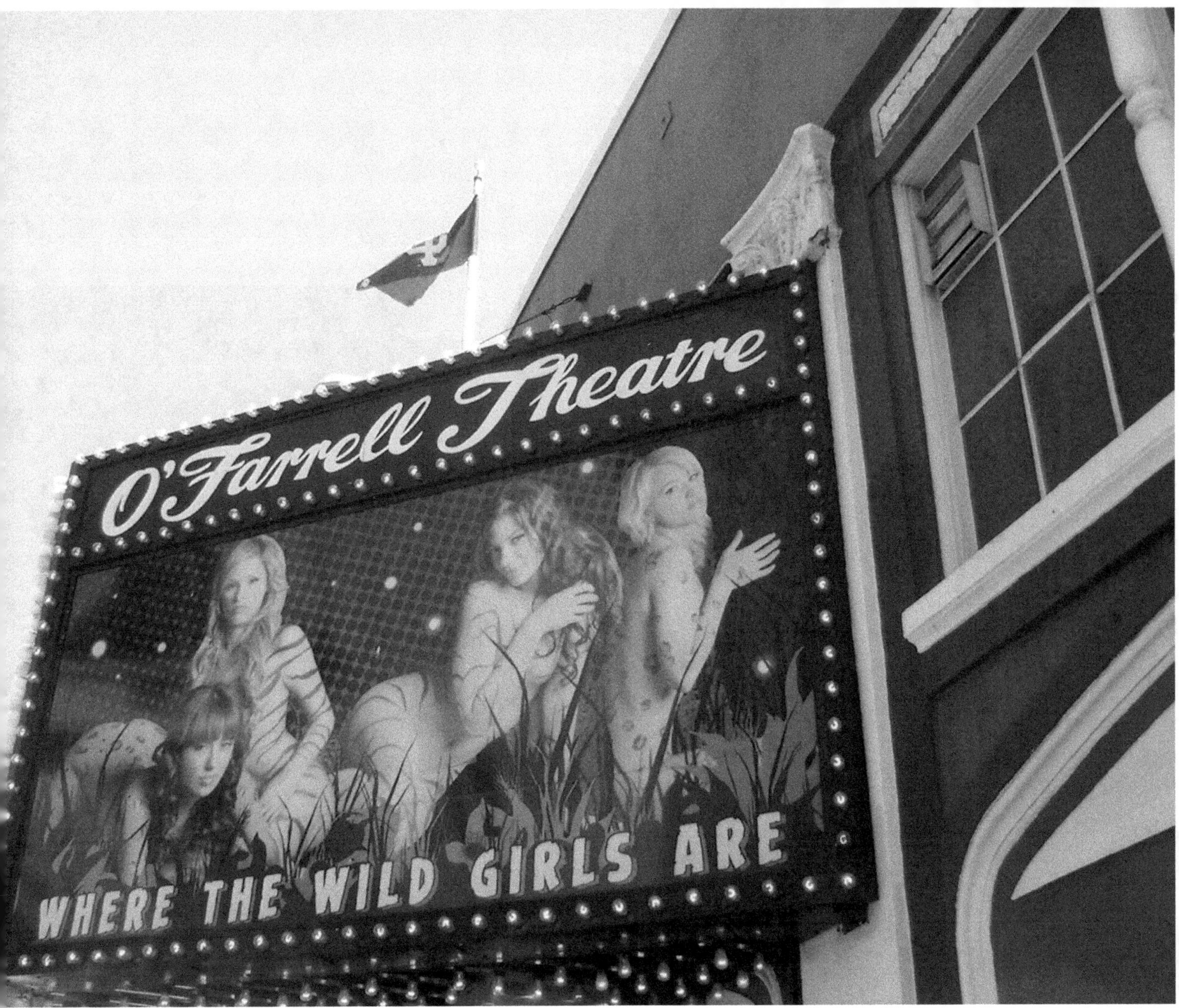
O'Farrell Theatre
WHERE THE WILD GIRLS ARE

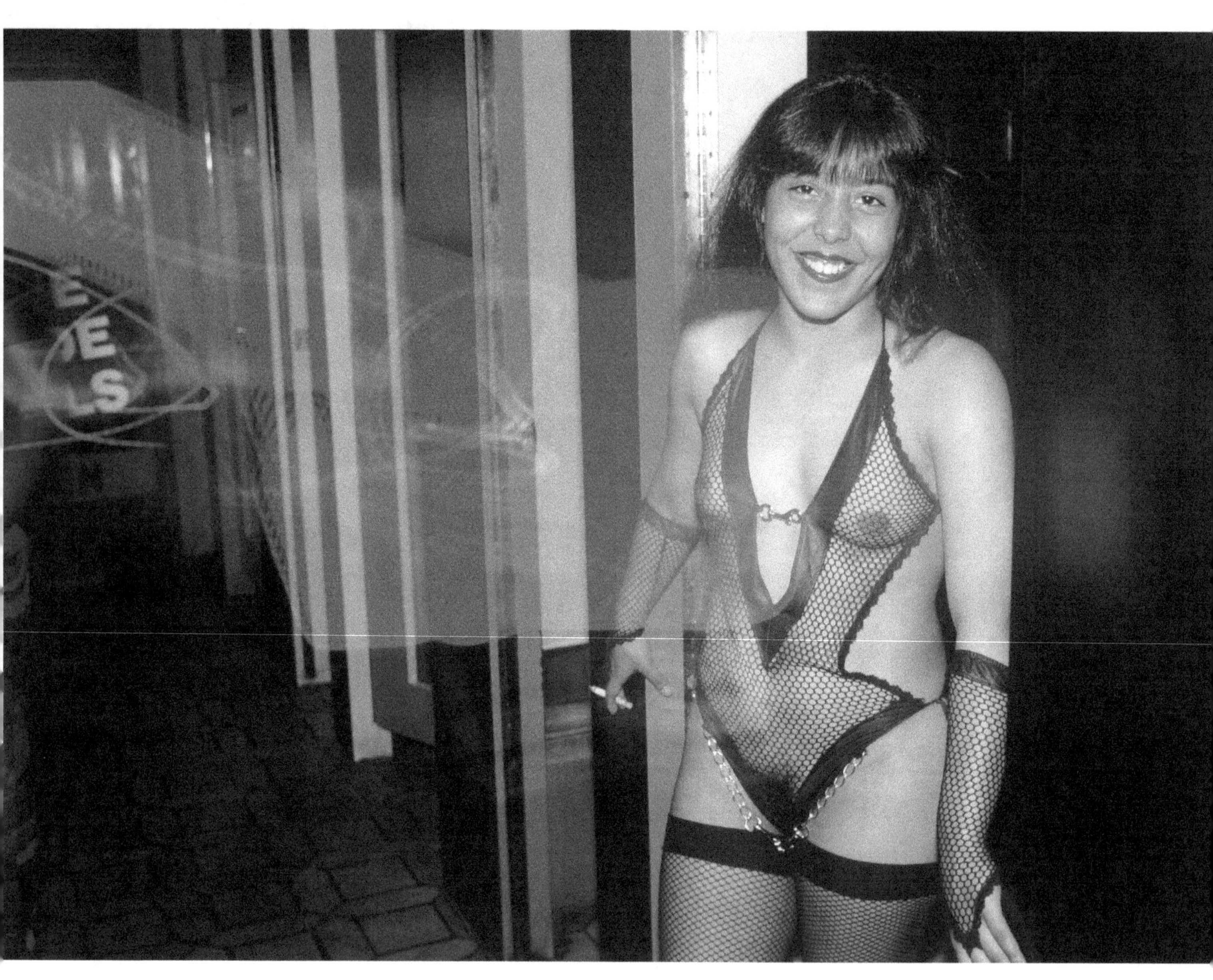

This Space for Rent

Bodies felt.

Perfumed,
rubbed,
pricked,
massaged,
poked,
hurt,
cleaned,
pinched,
aching,
soiled,
tingling.

Bodies for rent.

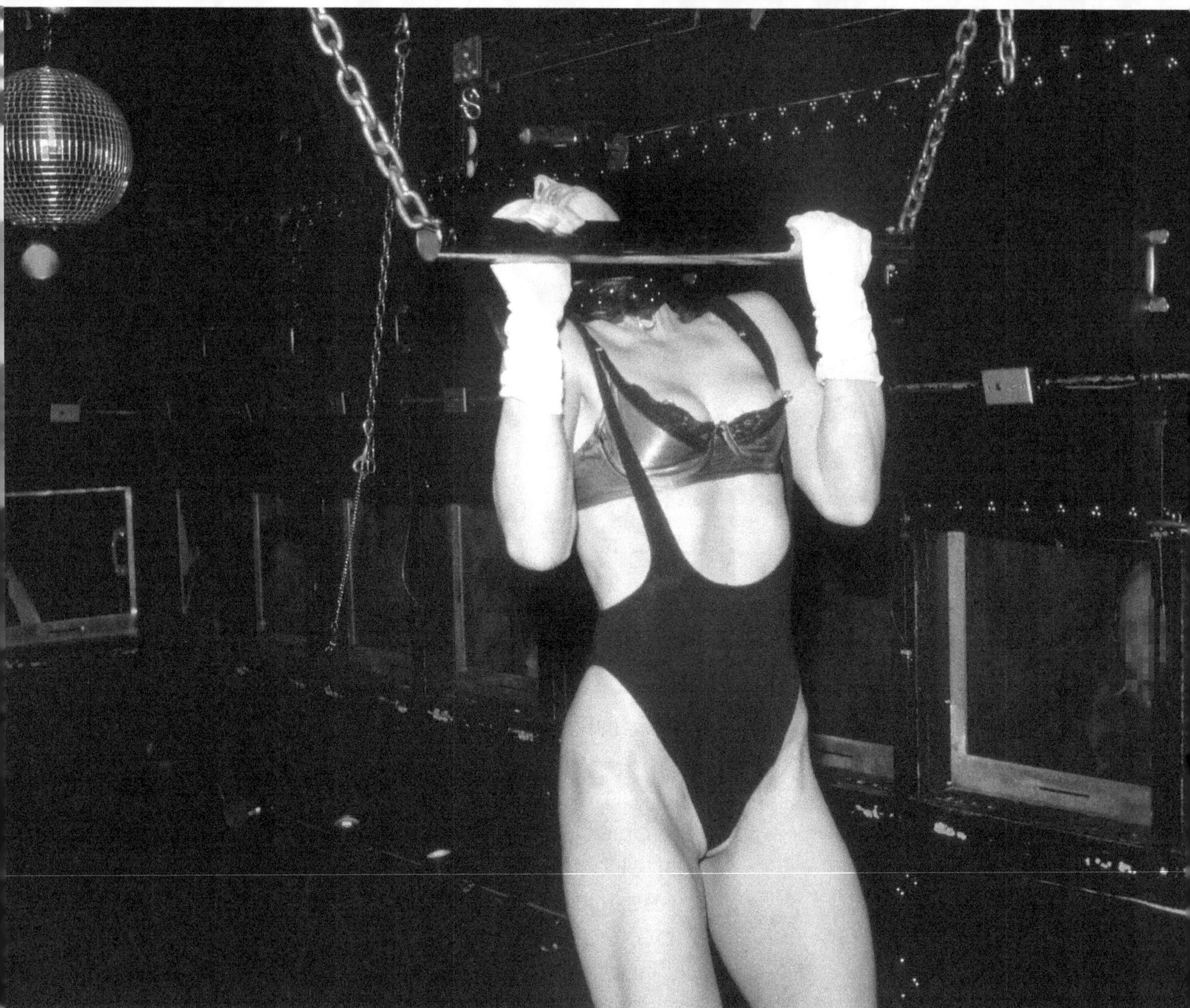

Dark Theatre

Women are
toys of the dark.

Theatre, bottomless dark.

Bottomless panties,
bottomless pitch,
dark.

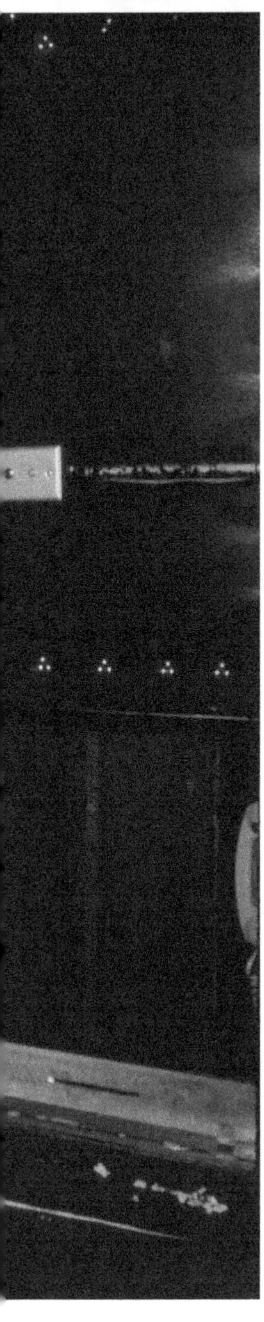

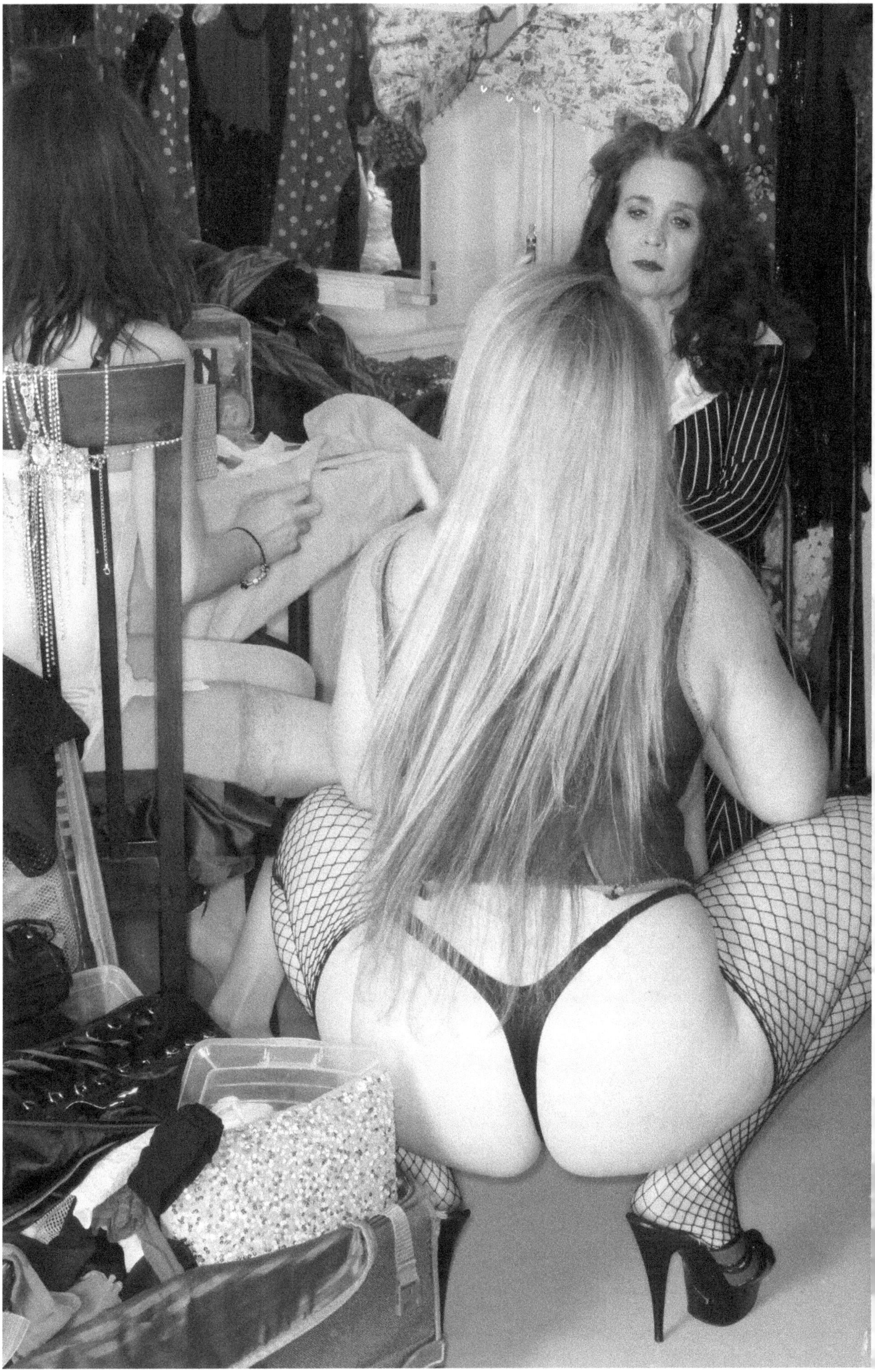

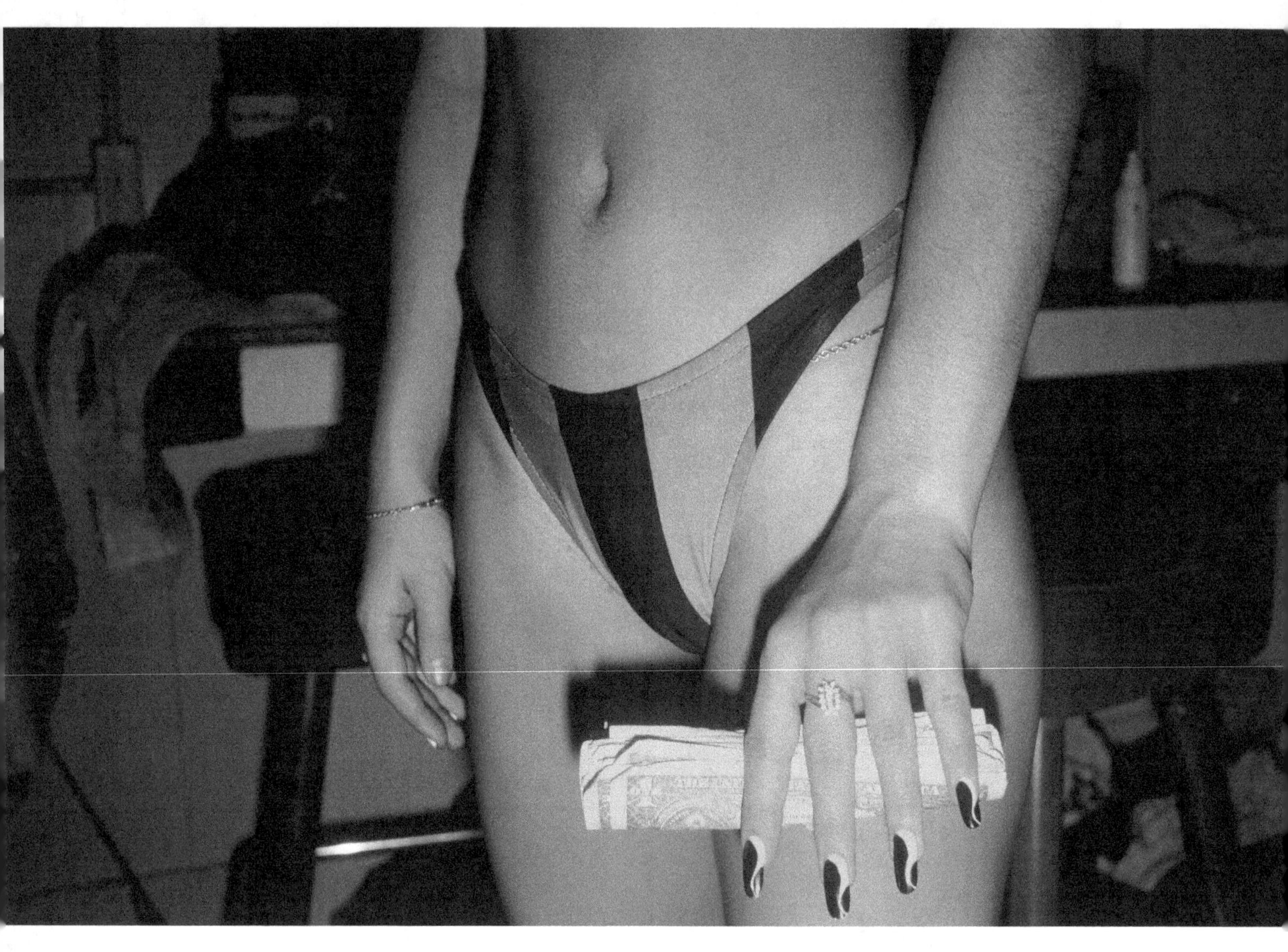

Money, Honey

Money
for makeup,
for costumes.
I gotta pay
the rent.

I need
drugs
to make it all
bearable.

Here We Are

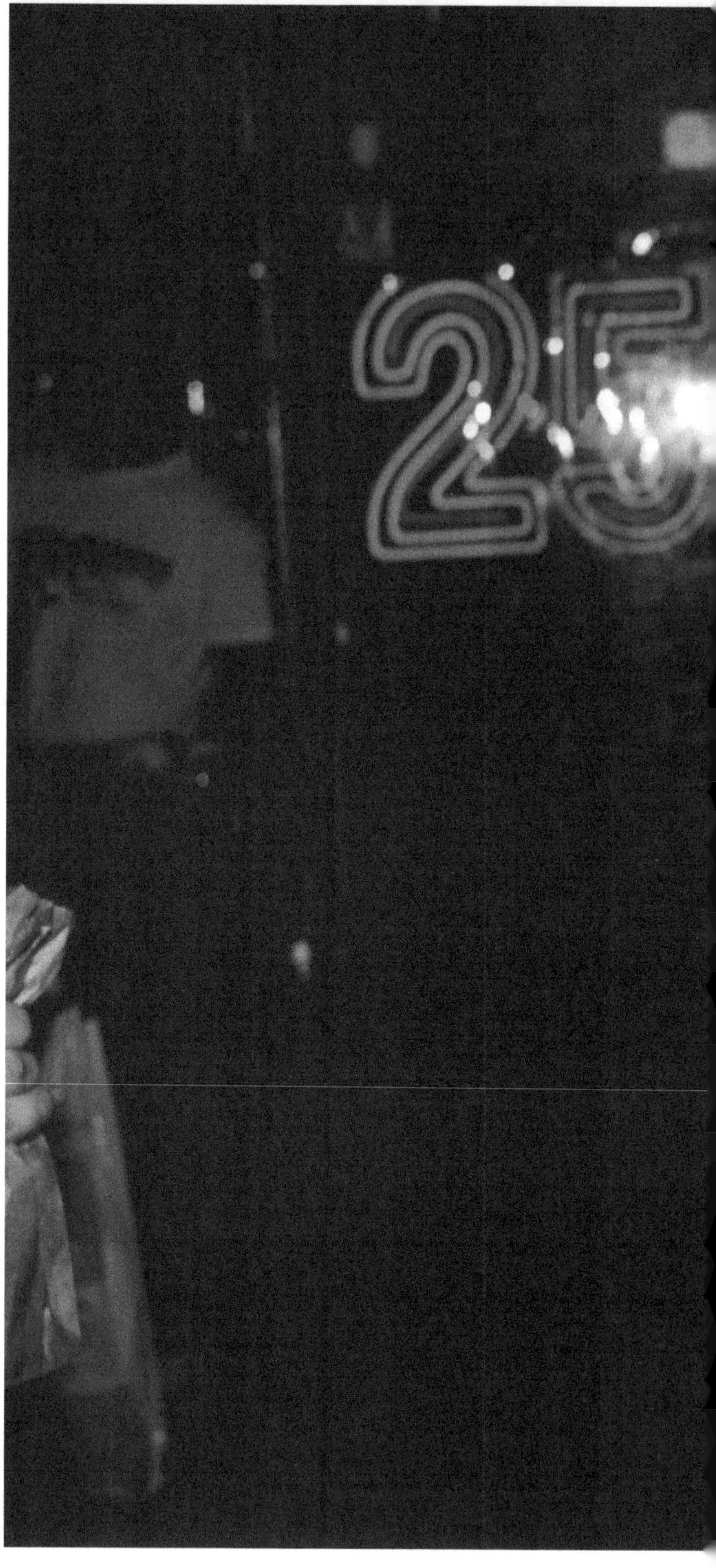

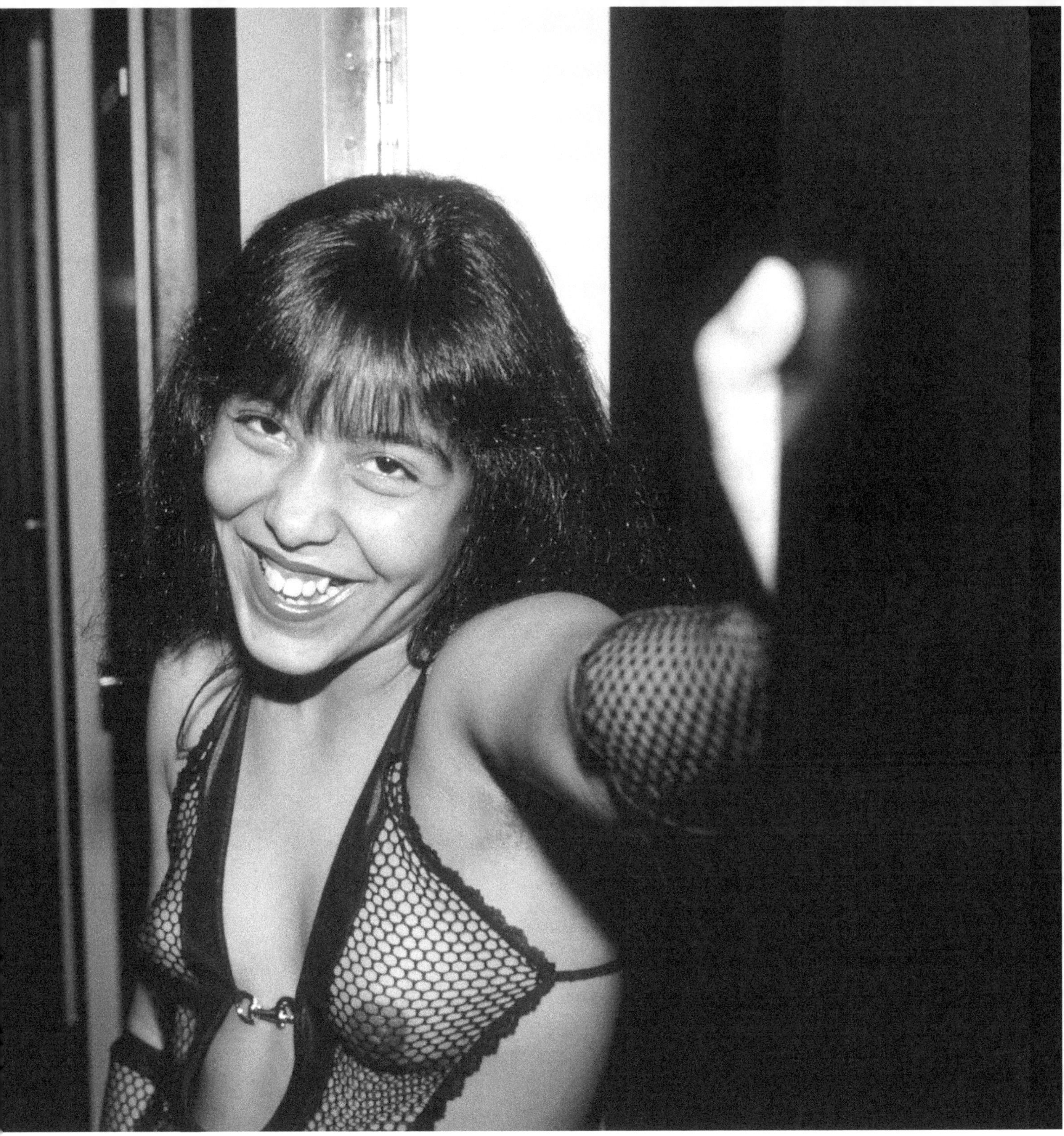

Here we are
for you:
a fake smile.

We are chilled
beneath the warm flesh.

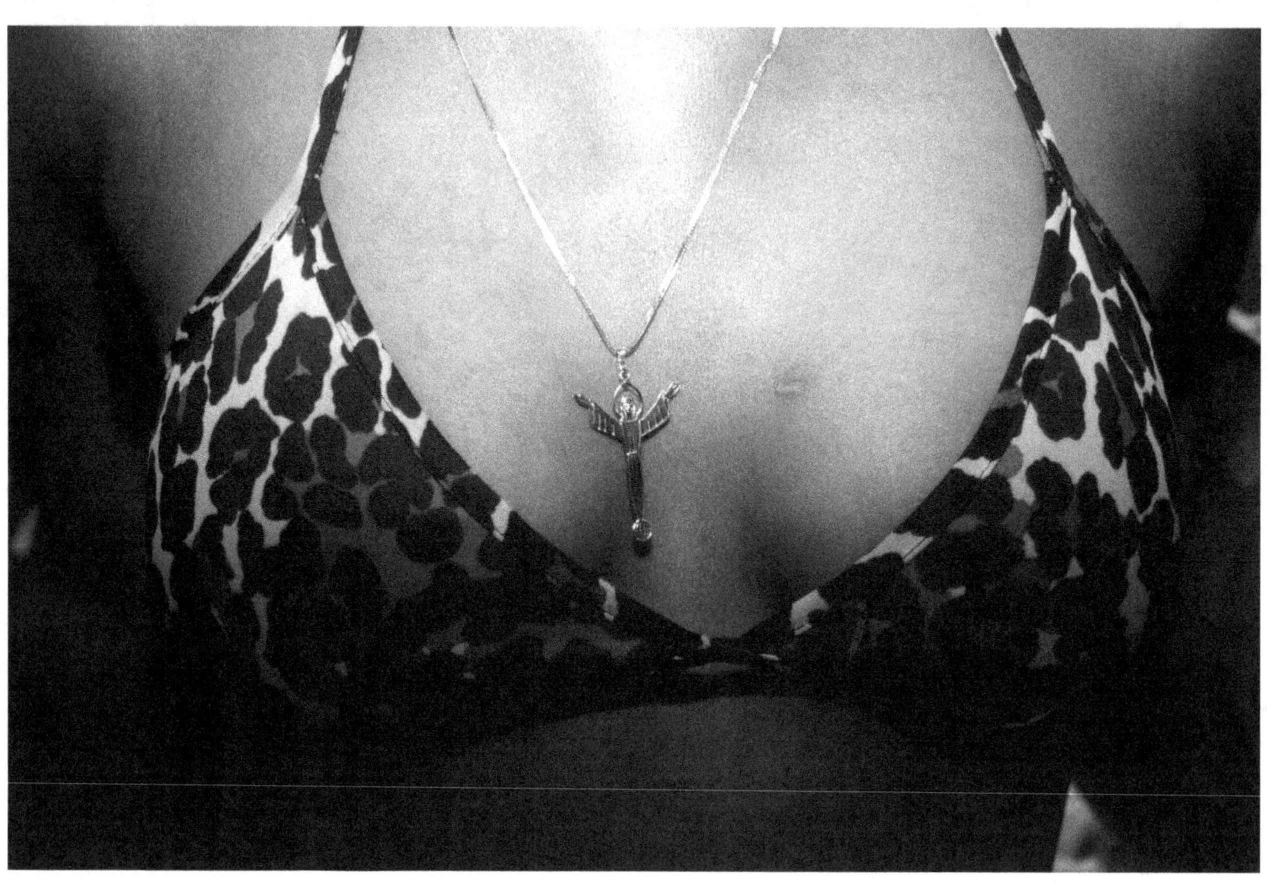

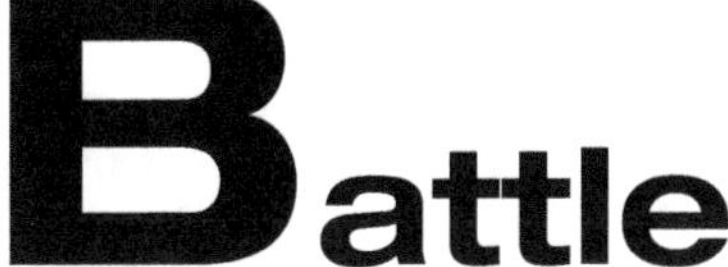

Battle

They have gotten
used to us.

We have gotten
used by them.

Benign battle.

Minimum Wage

They are icebergs
drowning themselves:
they'll give you only a tip.

We make it on tips
and minimum wage.

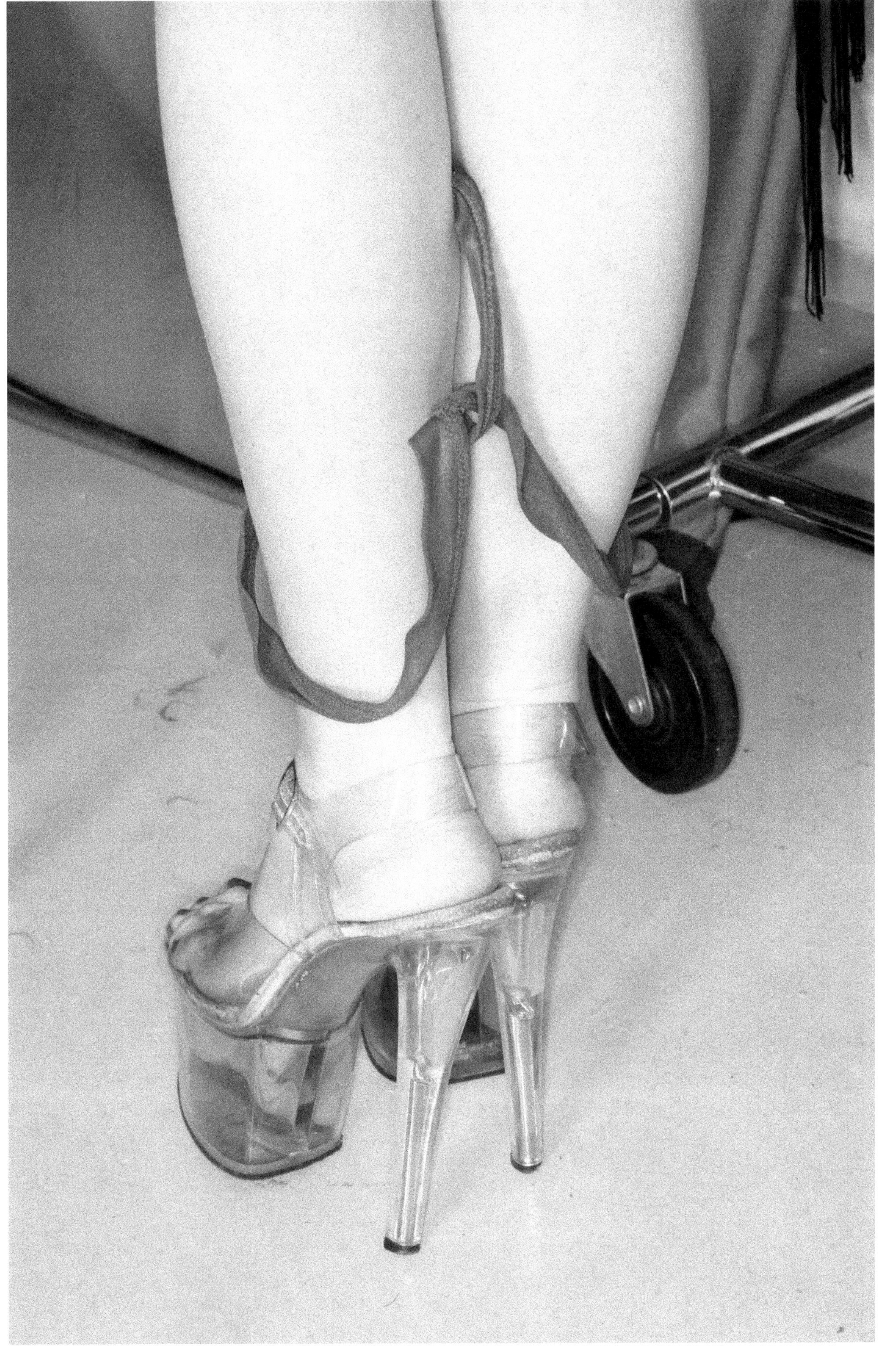

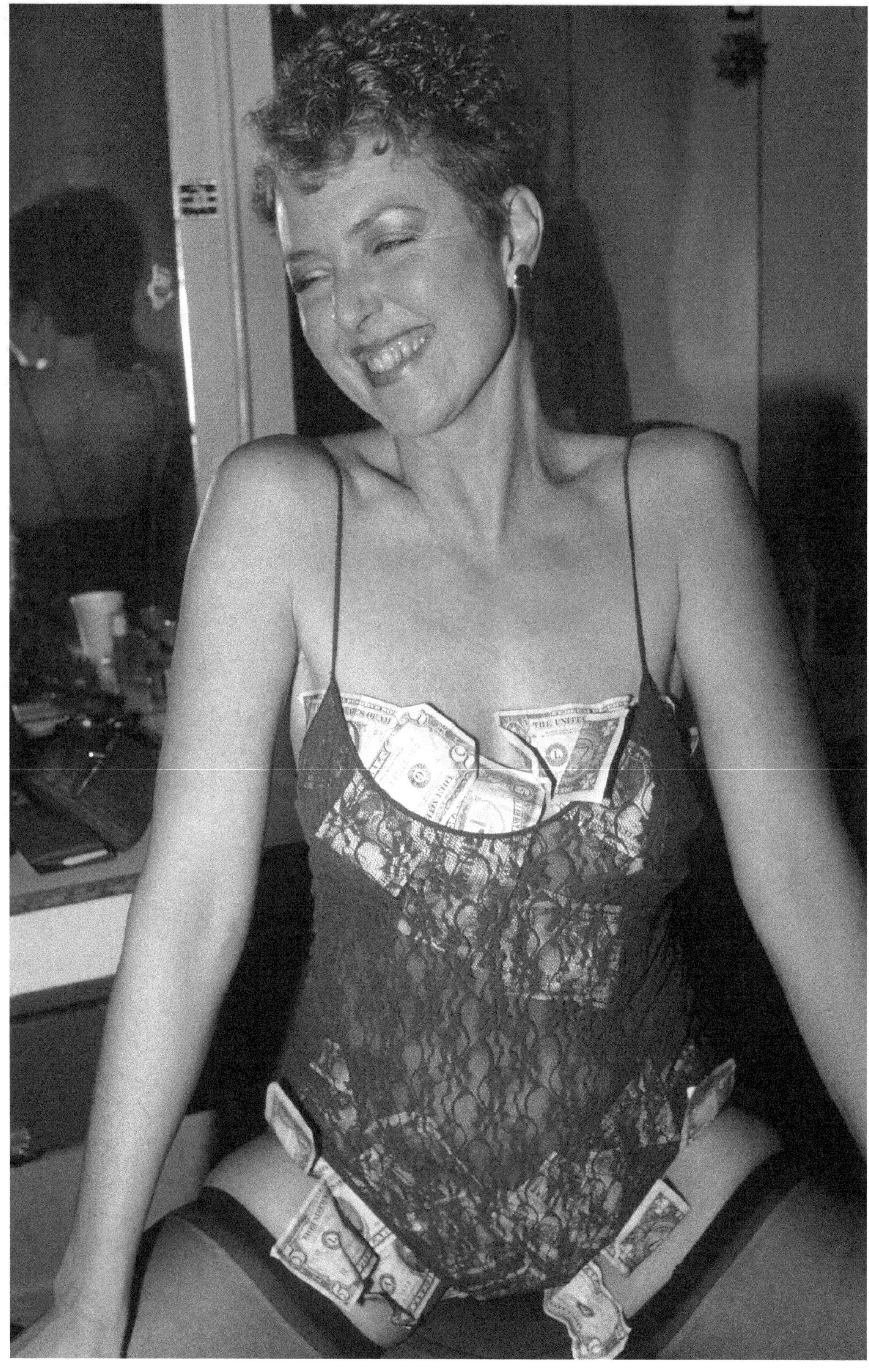

She Will Surrender

Bribe her,
she'll come close.

Hollowed-eyed creature,
give her money.

Lust corrupts,
the void surrounds.

She'll surrender to your wallet.

Fluff

Dancing's nice
and all that stuff
but don't forget
to check for fluff!

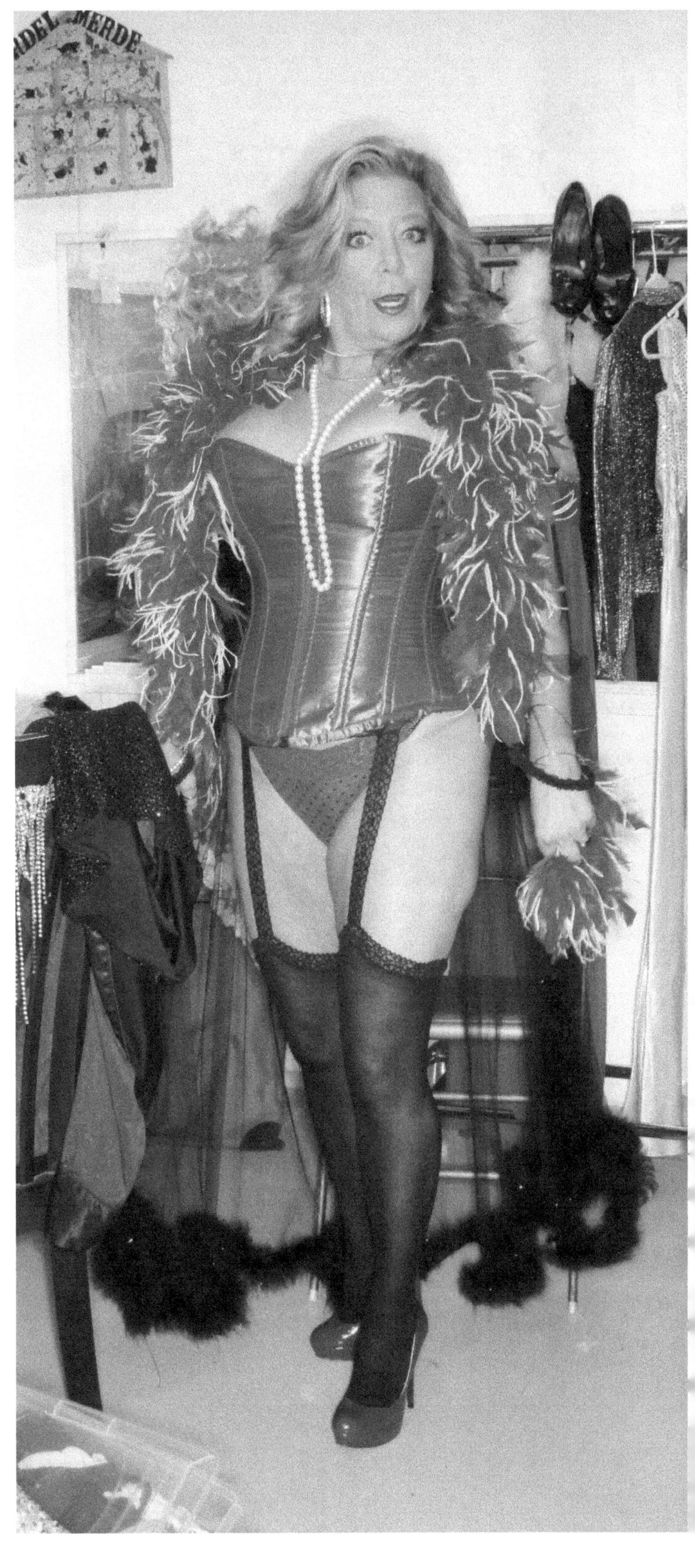

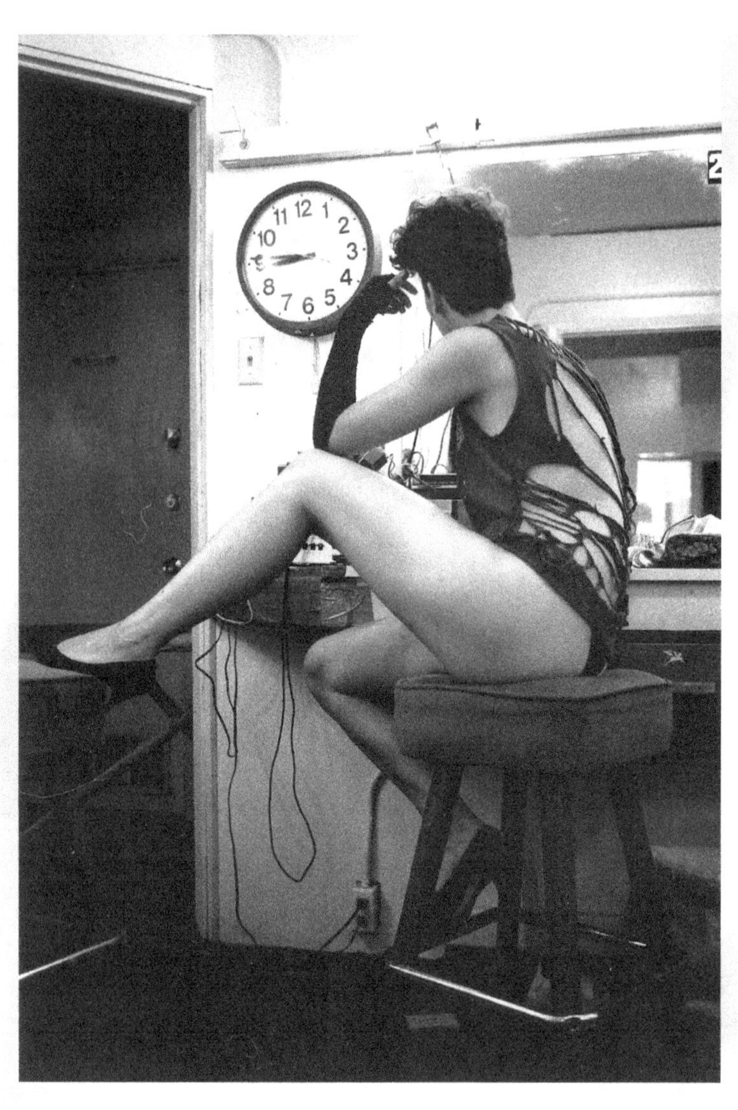

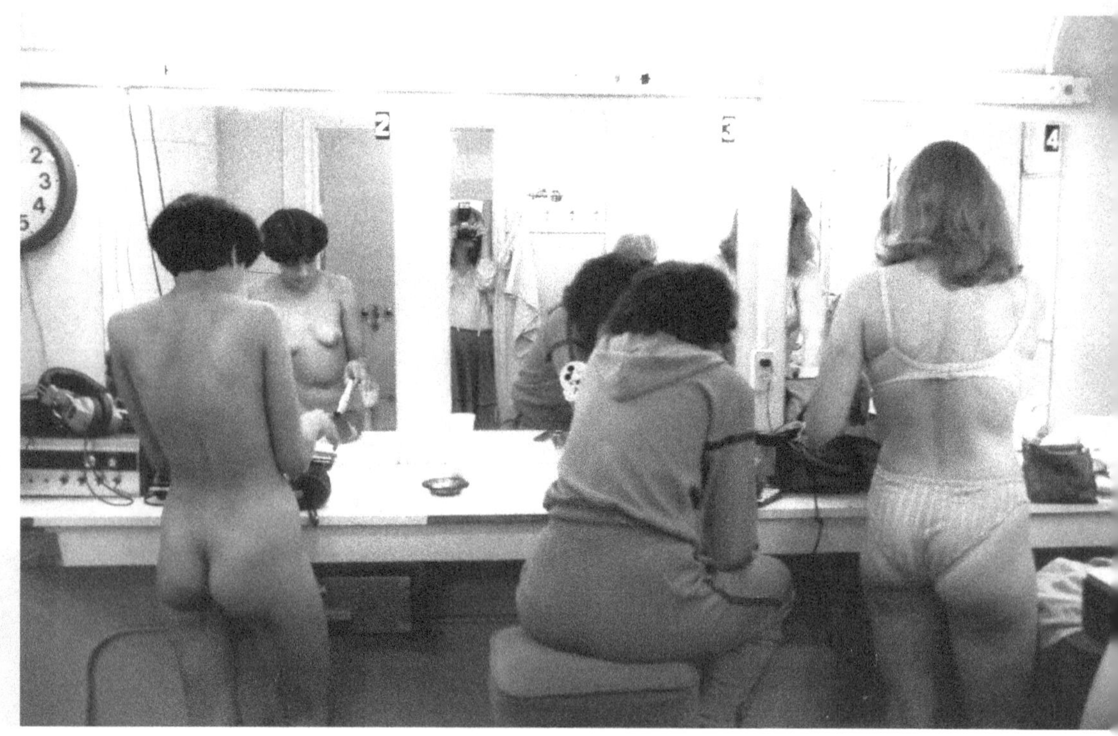

Time Clock

Time
clock
time.

Yet time
clicks.

Tick-tock...
Buzz.

Fish Tank

Body crawl.
Body shake.
Body thrust.

Body.

Body wave.

Body swimming
in the blue.

Fish tank
at O'Farrell
and Polk Street.

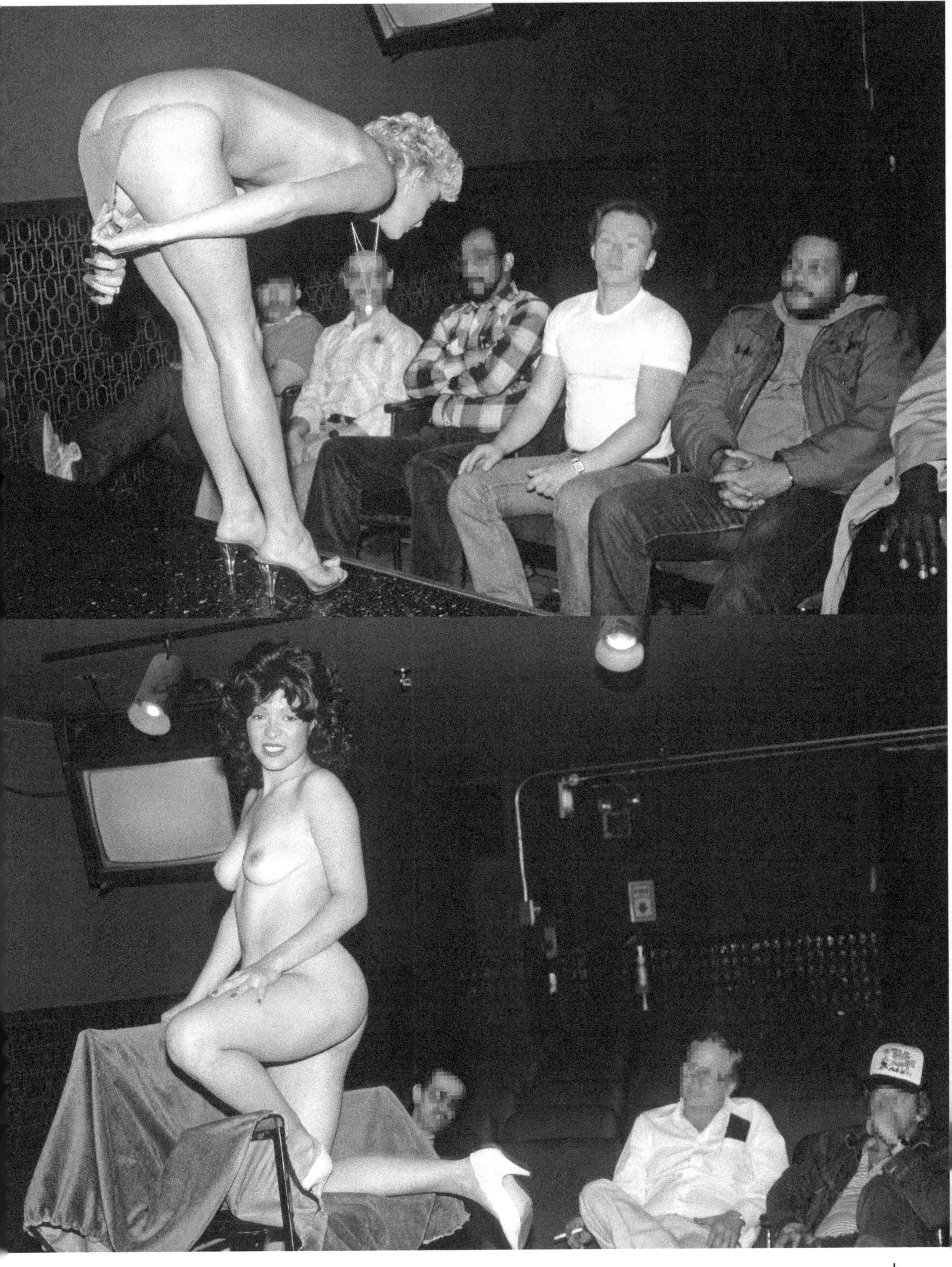

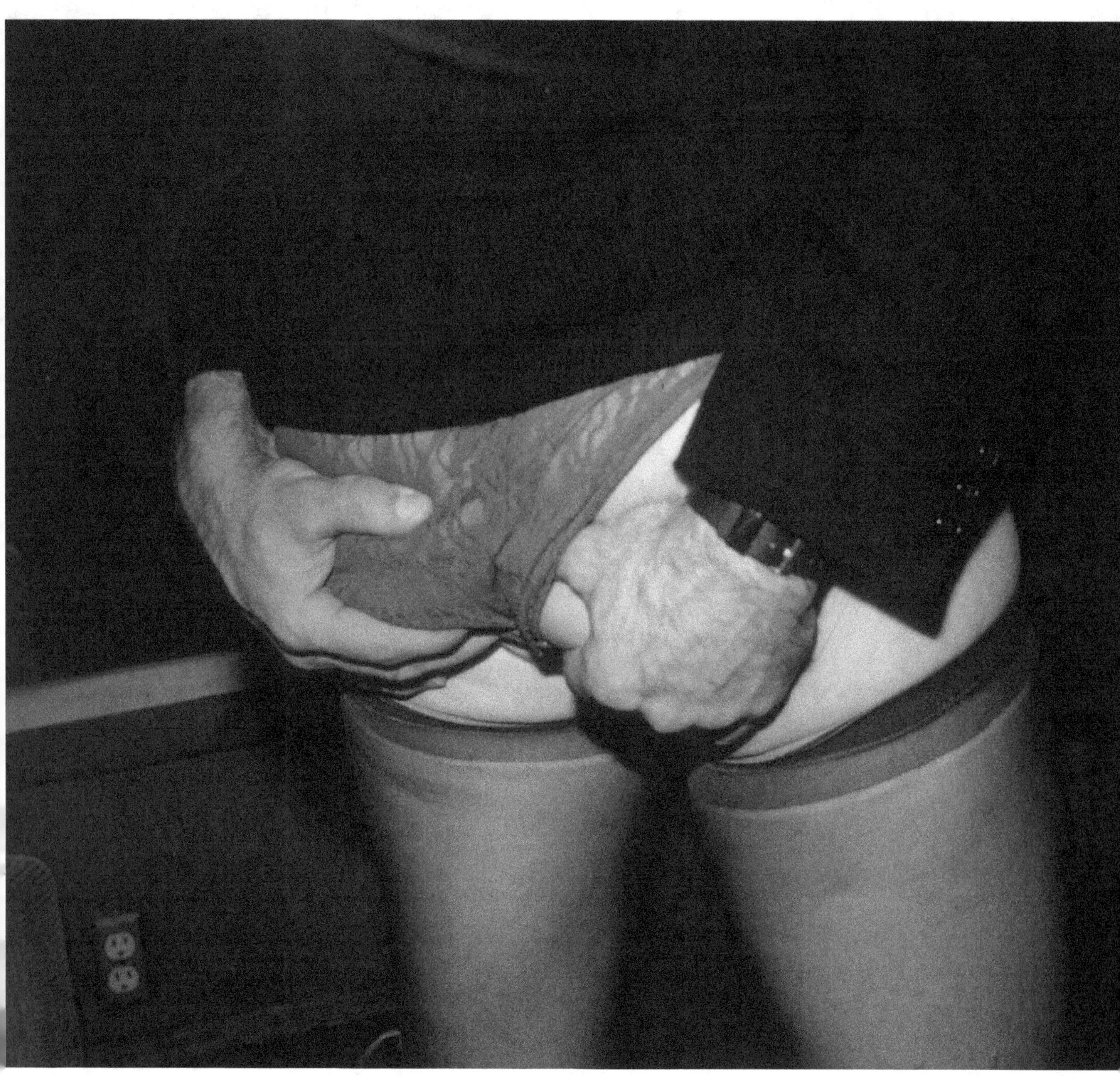

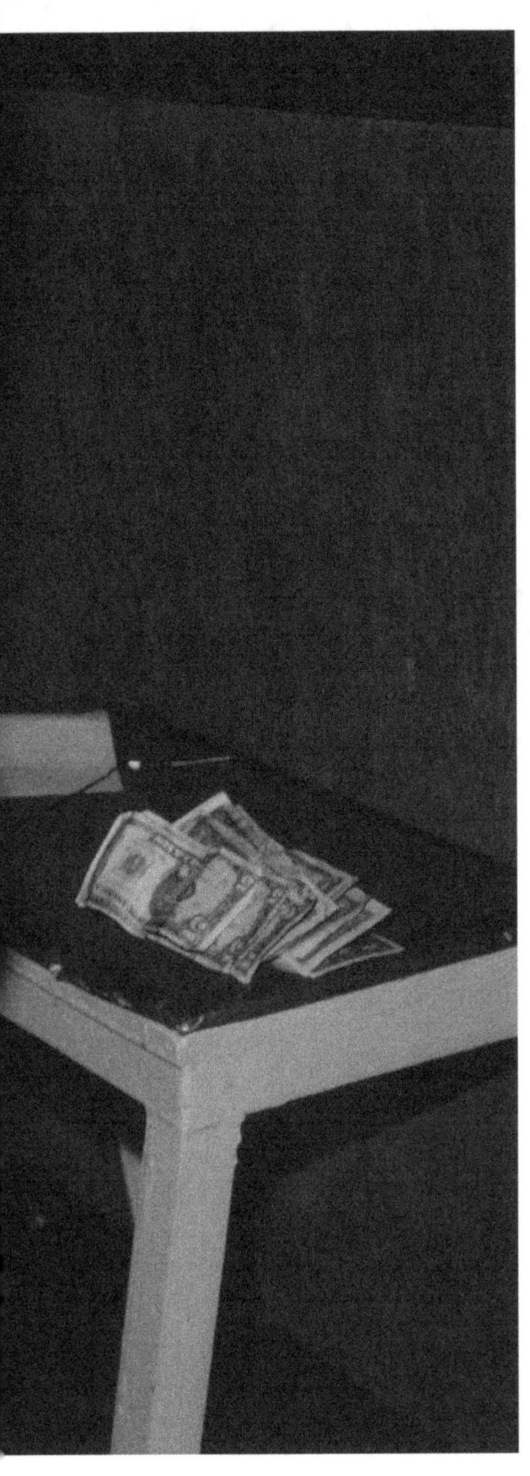

Money Talks

Money talks
when you talk
to me.

Put away
that single, honey.

Don't insult me.

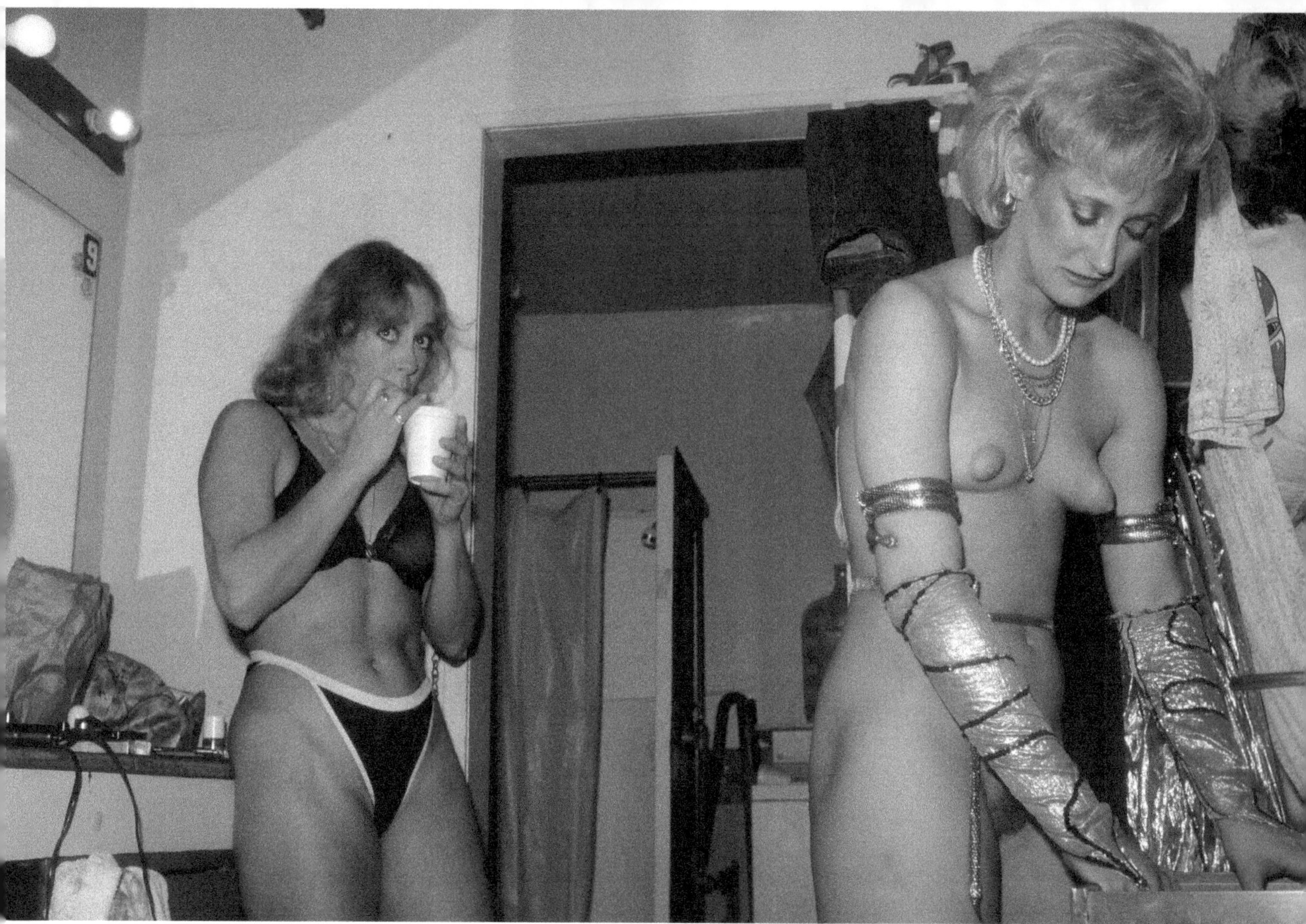

Dancing with No Pay

Dancing with No Pay
Dancing with No Pay
Dancing with No Pay
Dancing with No Pay
Dancing with No Pay
Dancing with No Pay
Dancing with No Pay

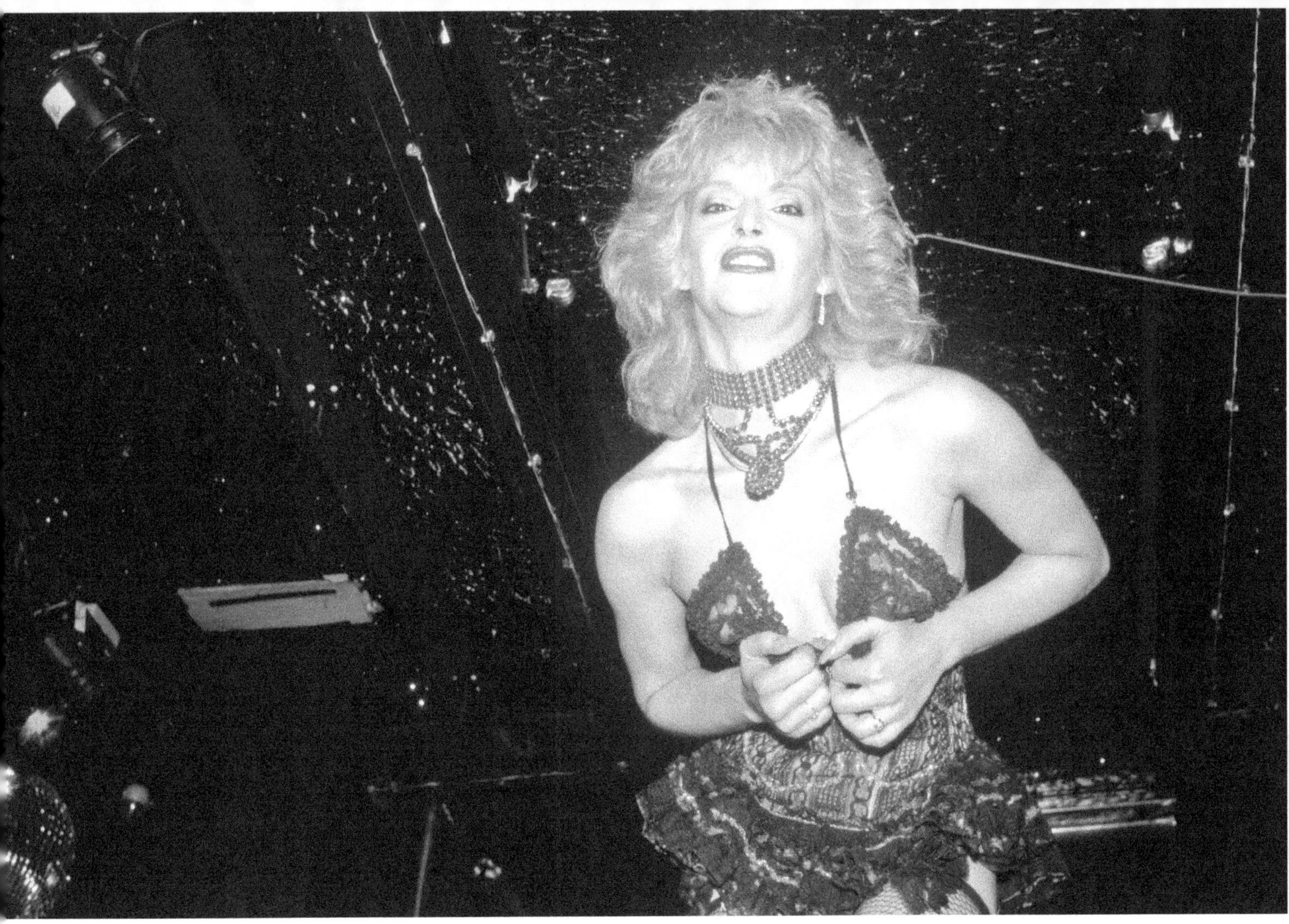

A dyke runs the lights
while her girlfriend dances.

Let's party!

Drunken junkie
falls off the stage,
and no one tries to catch her.

She goes home
without pay.

Bruise

Can I
cover this bruise?
Smile and chat?

What do you want?
You can forget that.

Give me a dollar
and let me go.

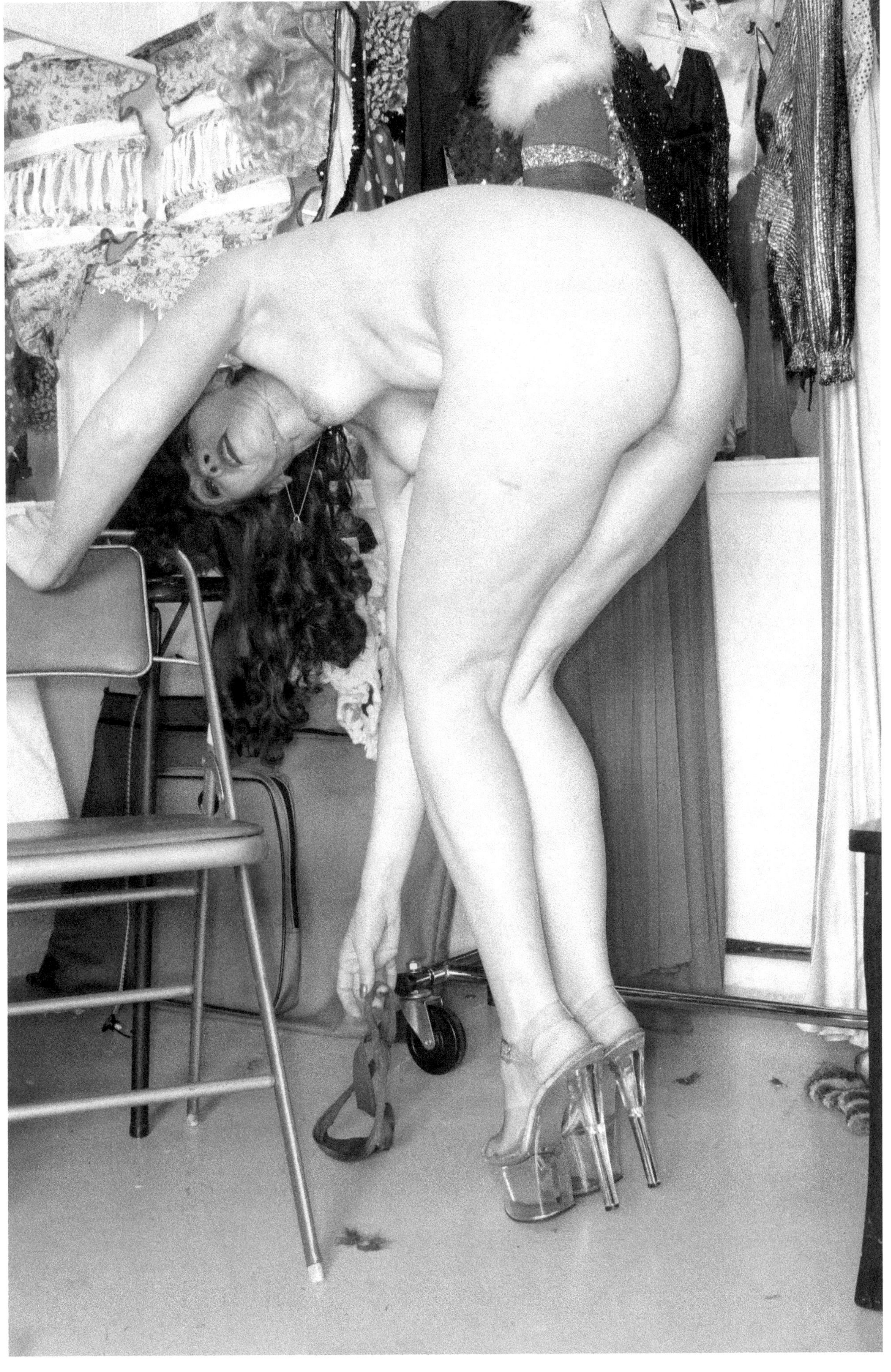

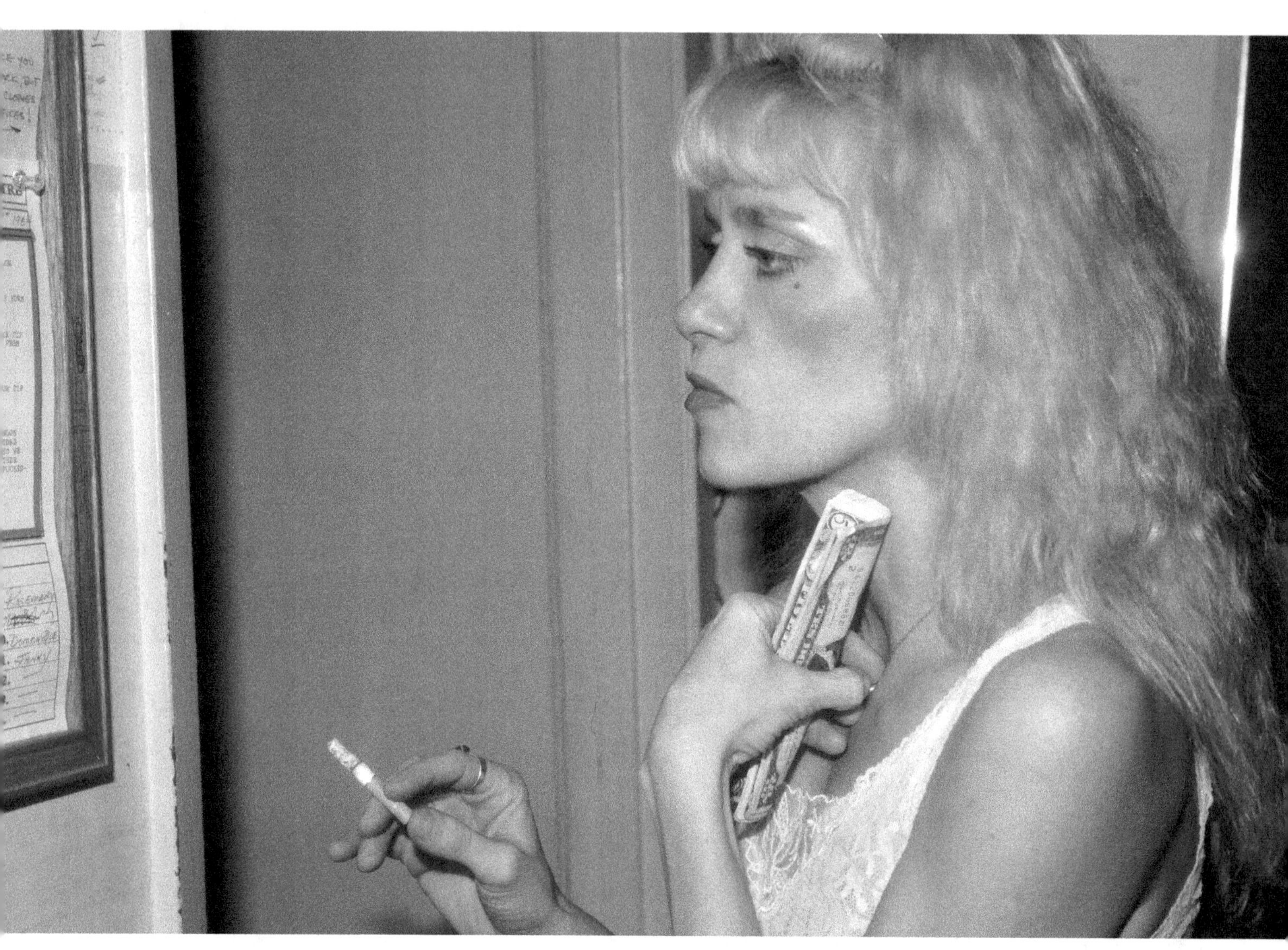

Purrs and Snuggles

Chain-smoking.
Drug-taking.
Eyes watering.
Curtain drawn.
Cat calls.

Purrs, snuggles and slaps.

A curl
falls over an eyebrow.

Mirror ball throws light about the
cave.

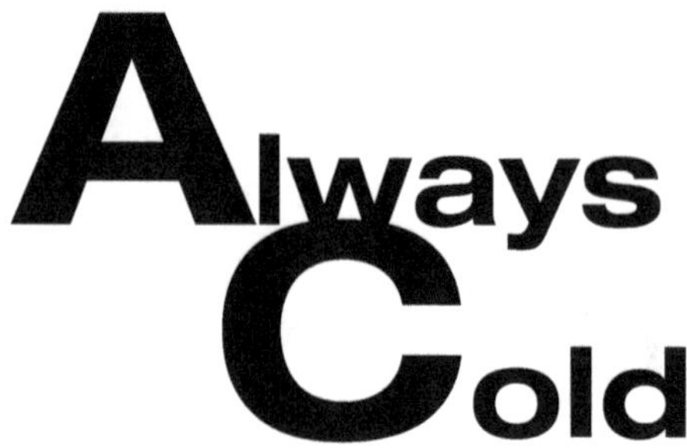

Always Cold

We are always cold, cold.
No telling why—just cold.

A hot shower before I dress.
My blood needs movement.
My body wants love,
but doesn't get it.

Stomach empty, just smoke more.

Long legs, tight pussy.
Famished soul.
Starving.

Imposters fill the seats.
Talk mingles,
becoming noise
and floats about my head
like smoke,
crowding thoughts into corners.

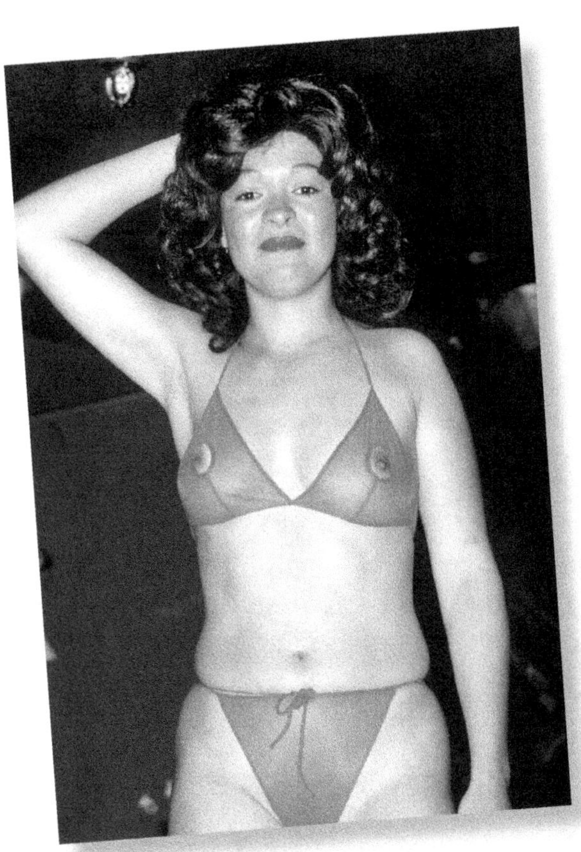

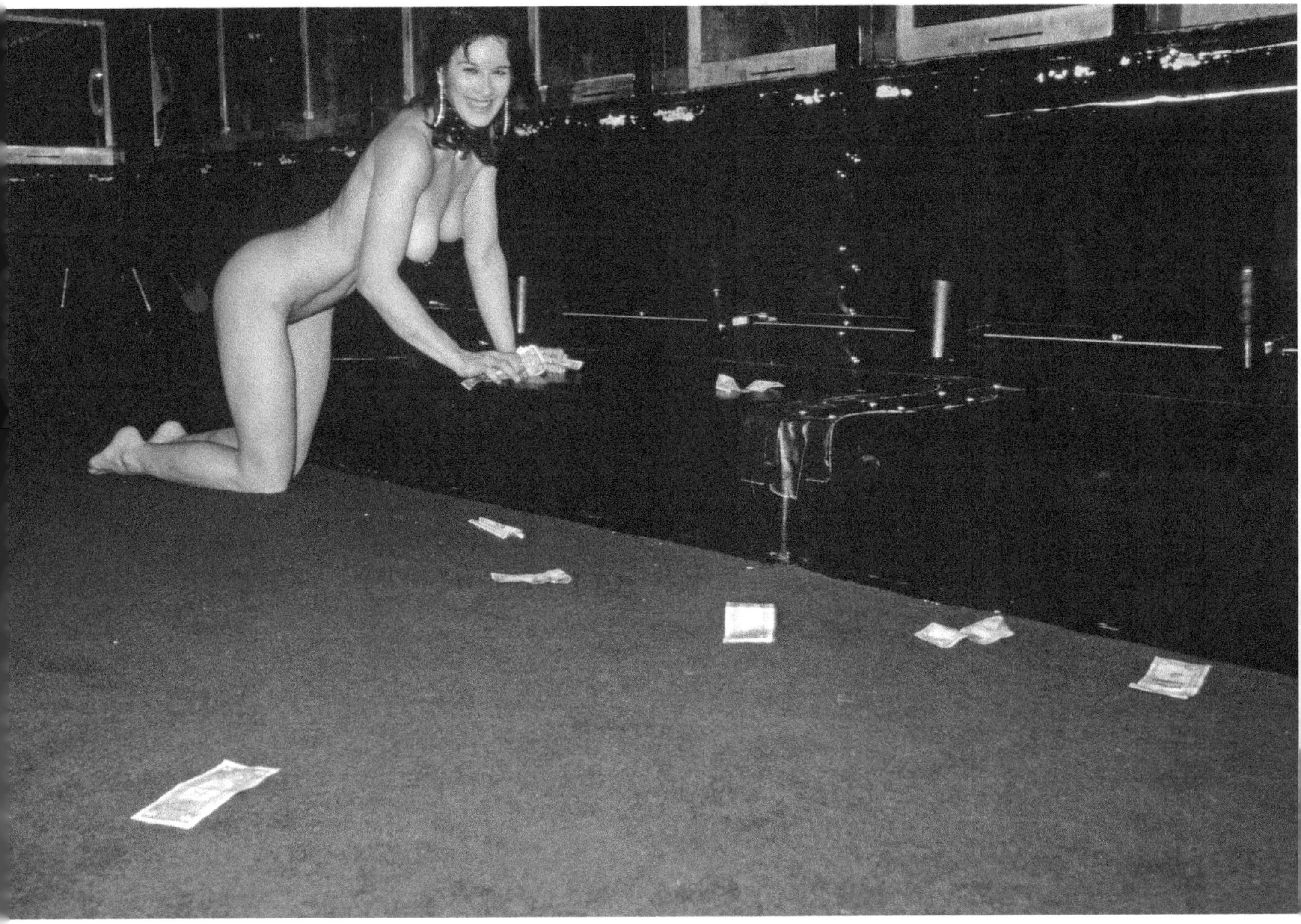

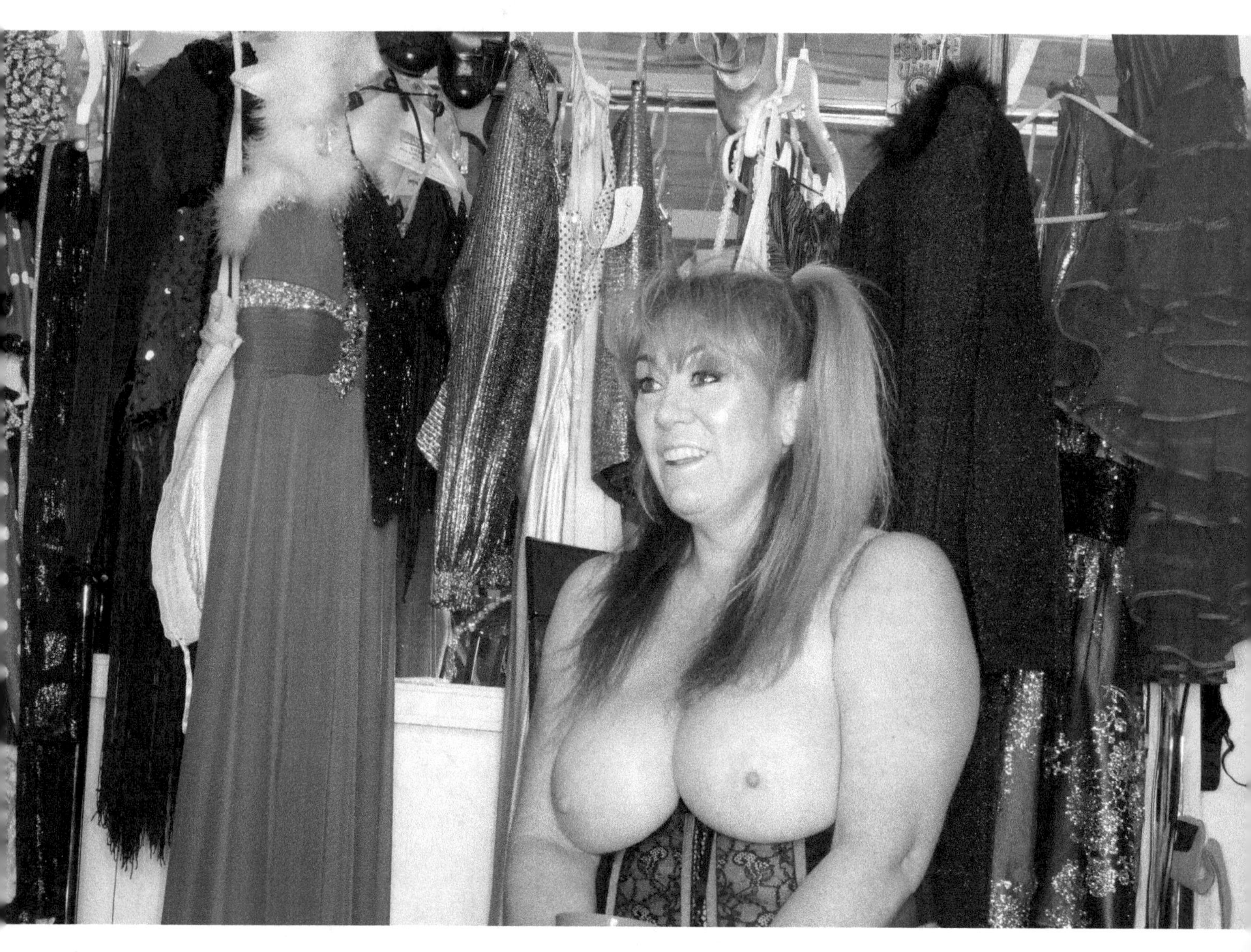

Cartoons

Cartoons of women,
dancers, whores,
thrill seekers.

They prance
and strut
onstage,
collapse
offstage.

Here, have some wine.

After...

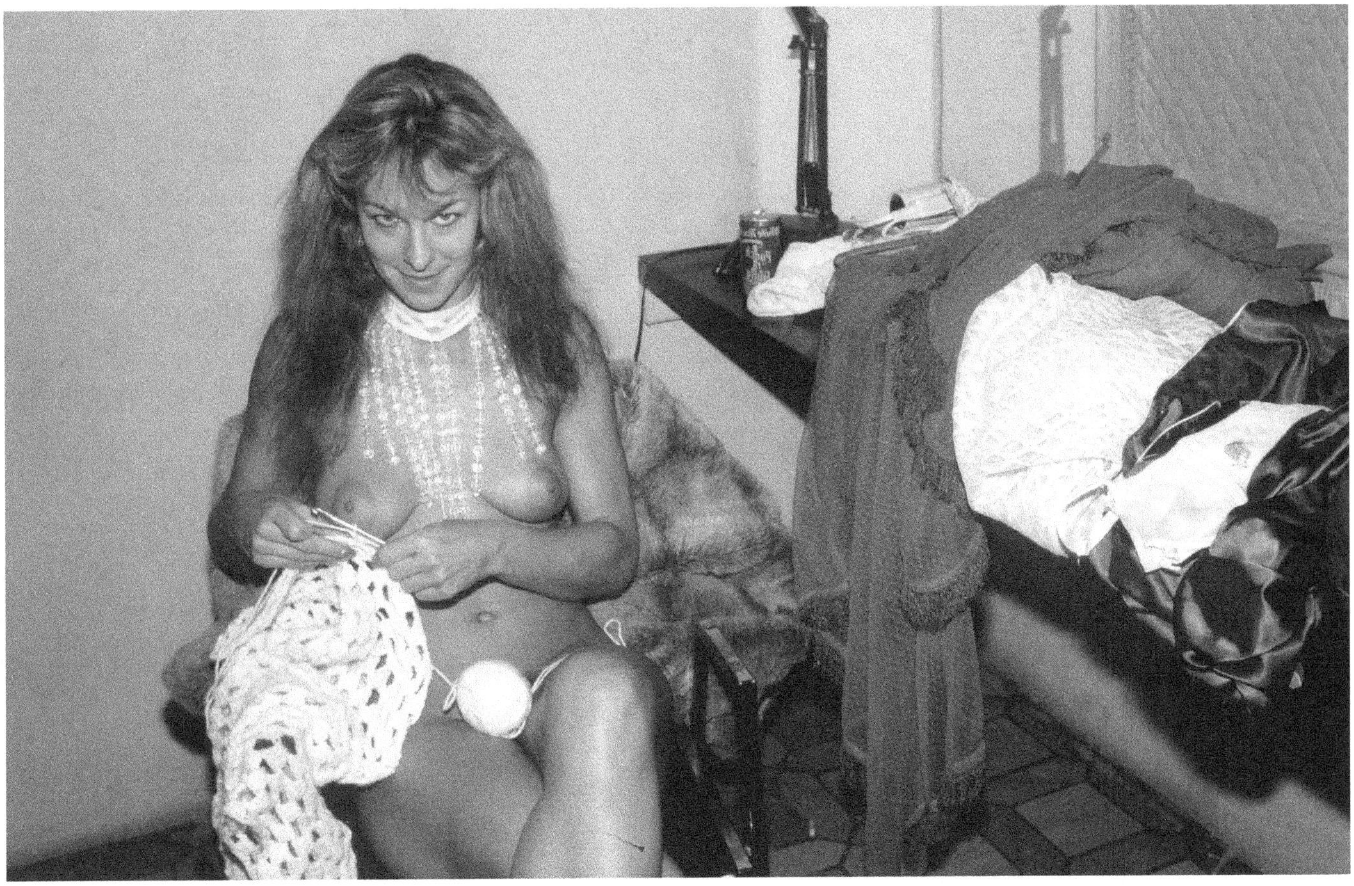

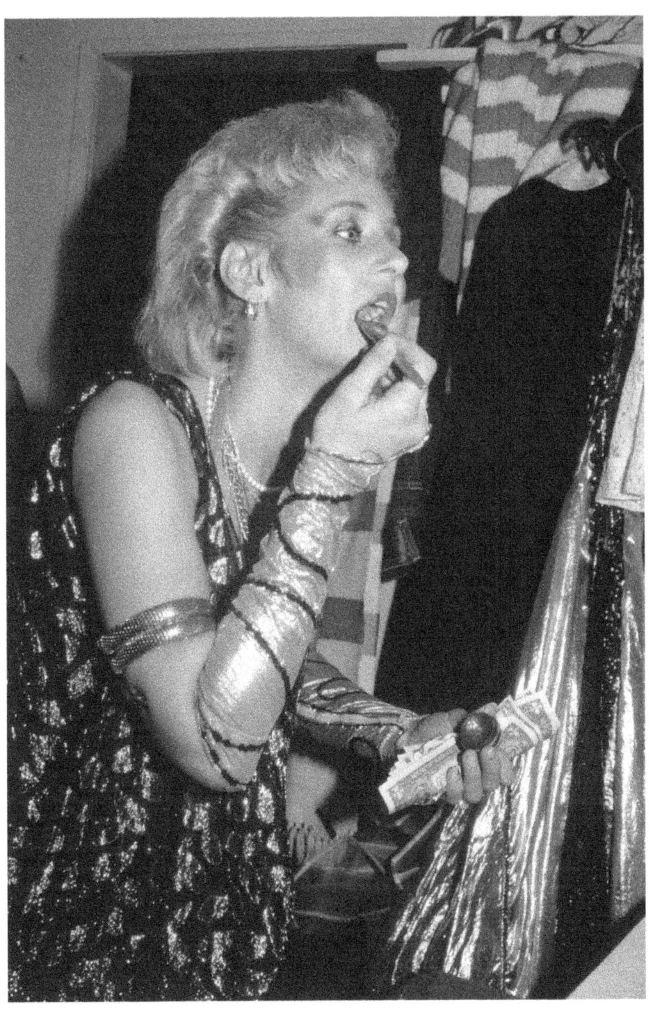

Spend That Dirty Money

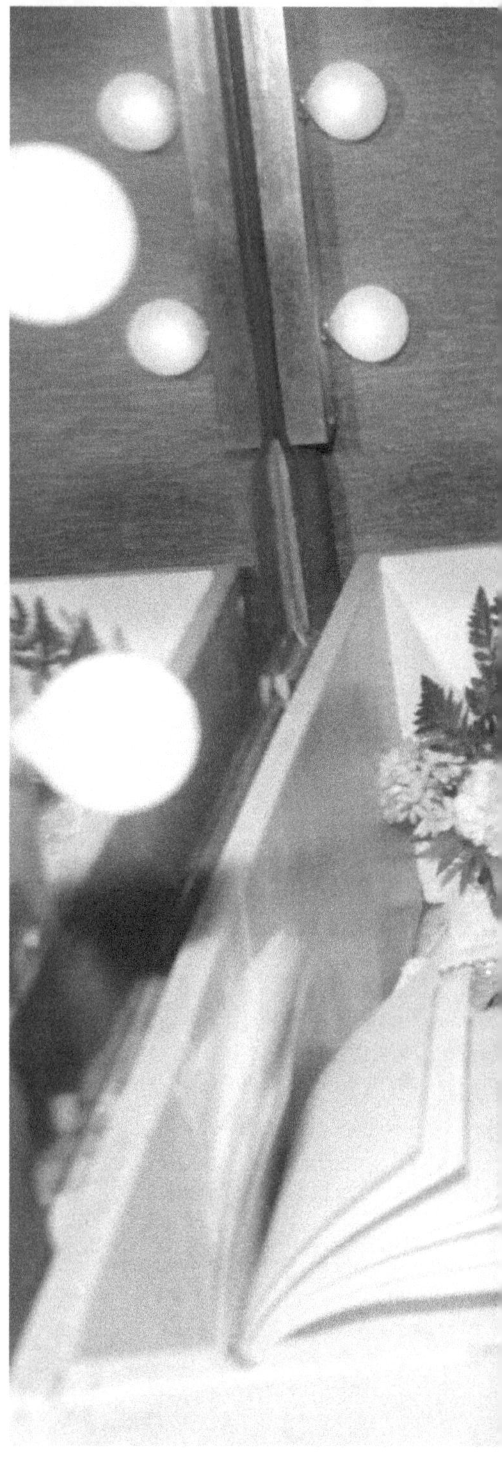

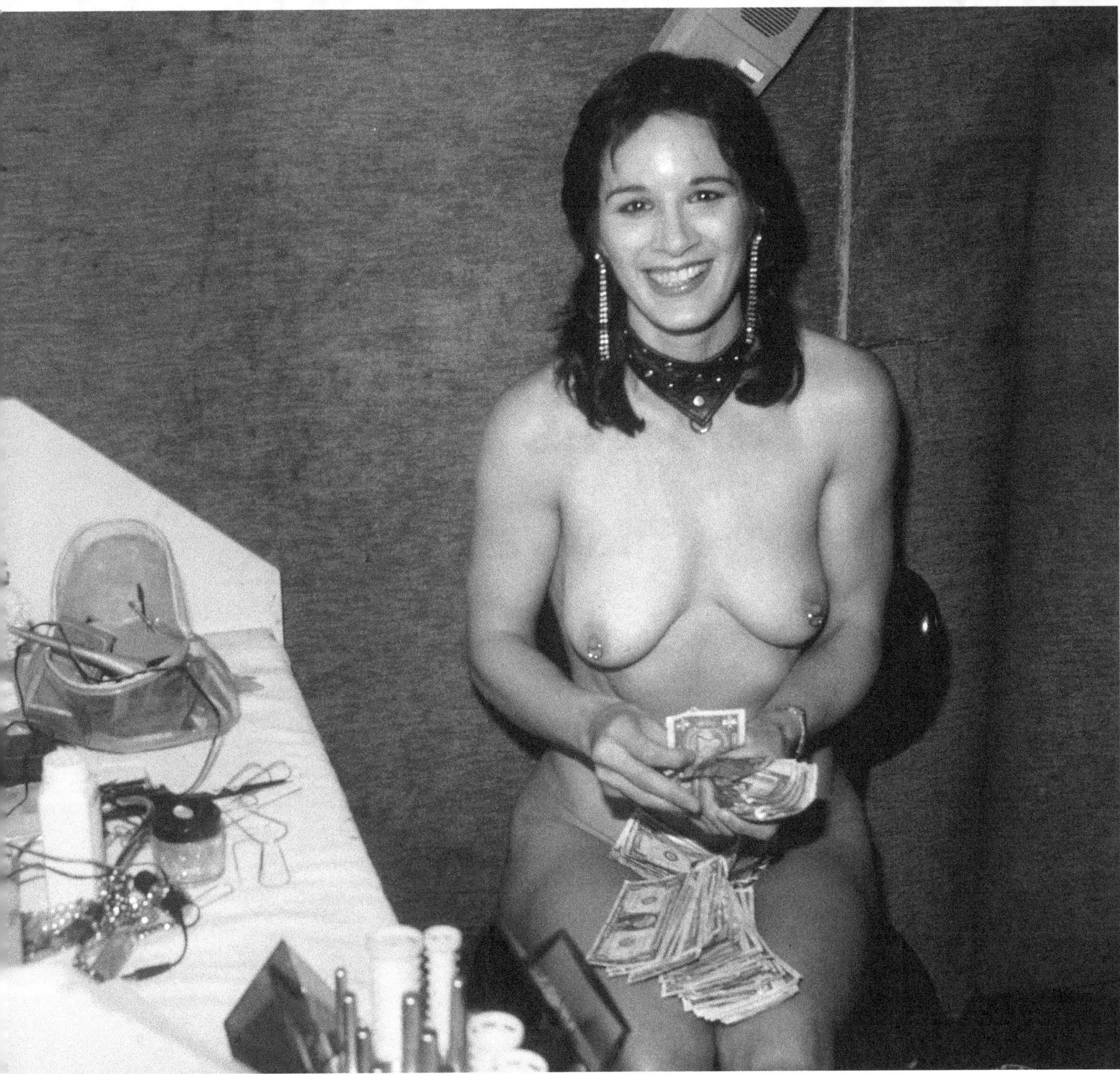

Dazed.
Gossip, lounge.
Complain, complain.
Count the money
Spend it quick.

Panting after the show.

Ladies of Always-Nite

Ladies of Always-Nite.

Twelve-hour shifts.

You'll never know
what kind of day
it has been.

You only know
how much pain
you hold.

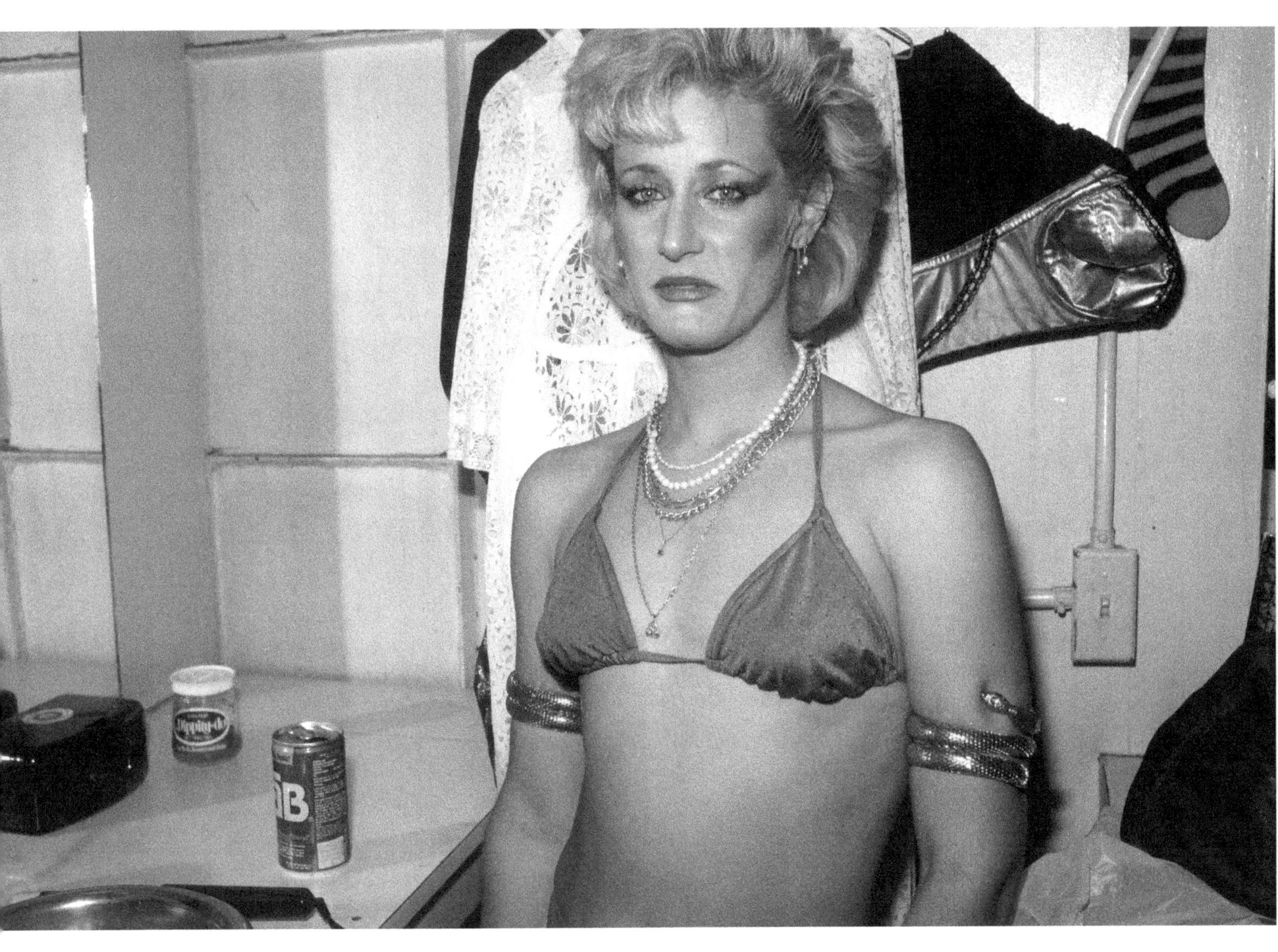

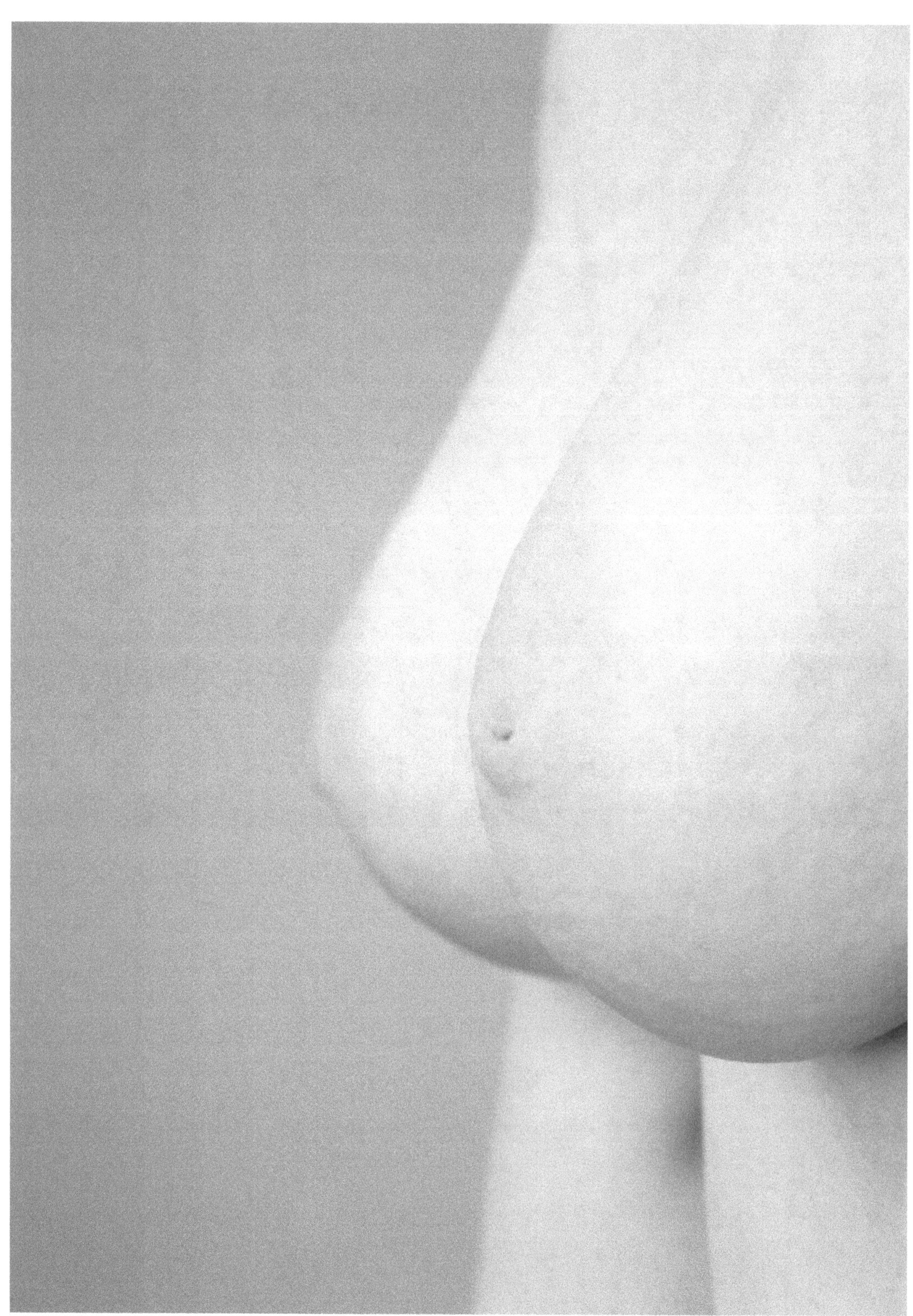

Through the Looking Glass

Looking glass looks.
Shattered panes.
Fantasy pains.

You are disgusting.
You are proud
You are meek.
Your tits are flushed,
hair mussed
through the looking glass.

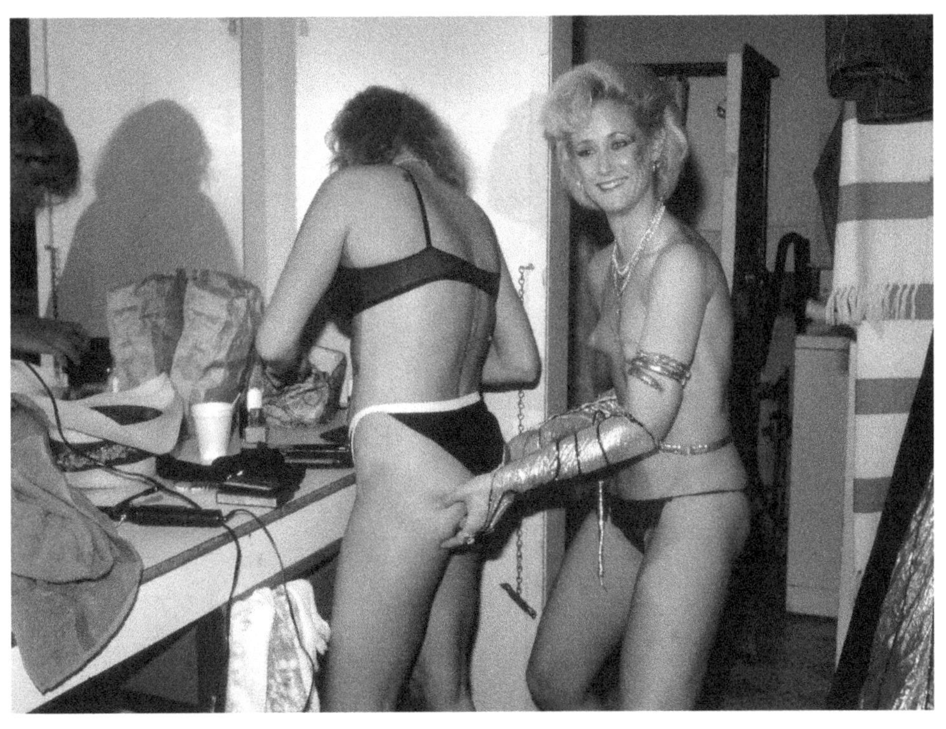

Chatter

Lazy chatter.
Latest fashions.
Old-time corsets.
New rock band.

Largest penis,
longest,
hardest.

Forget love.

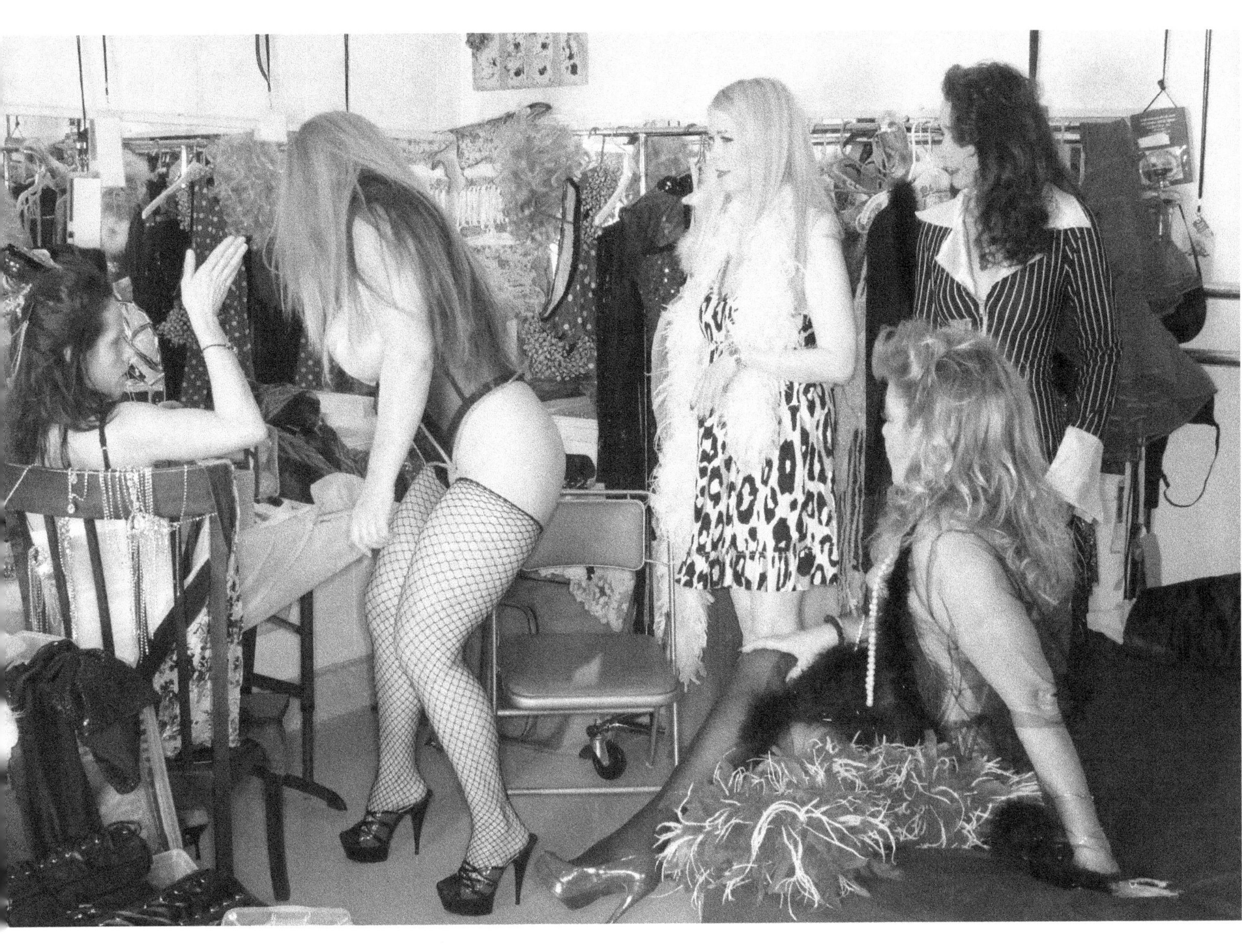

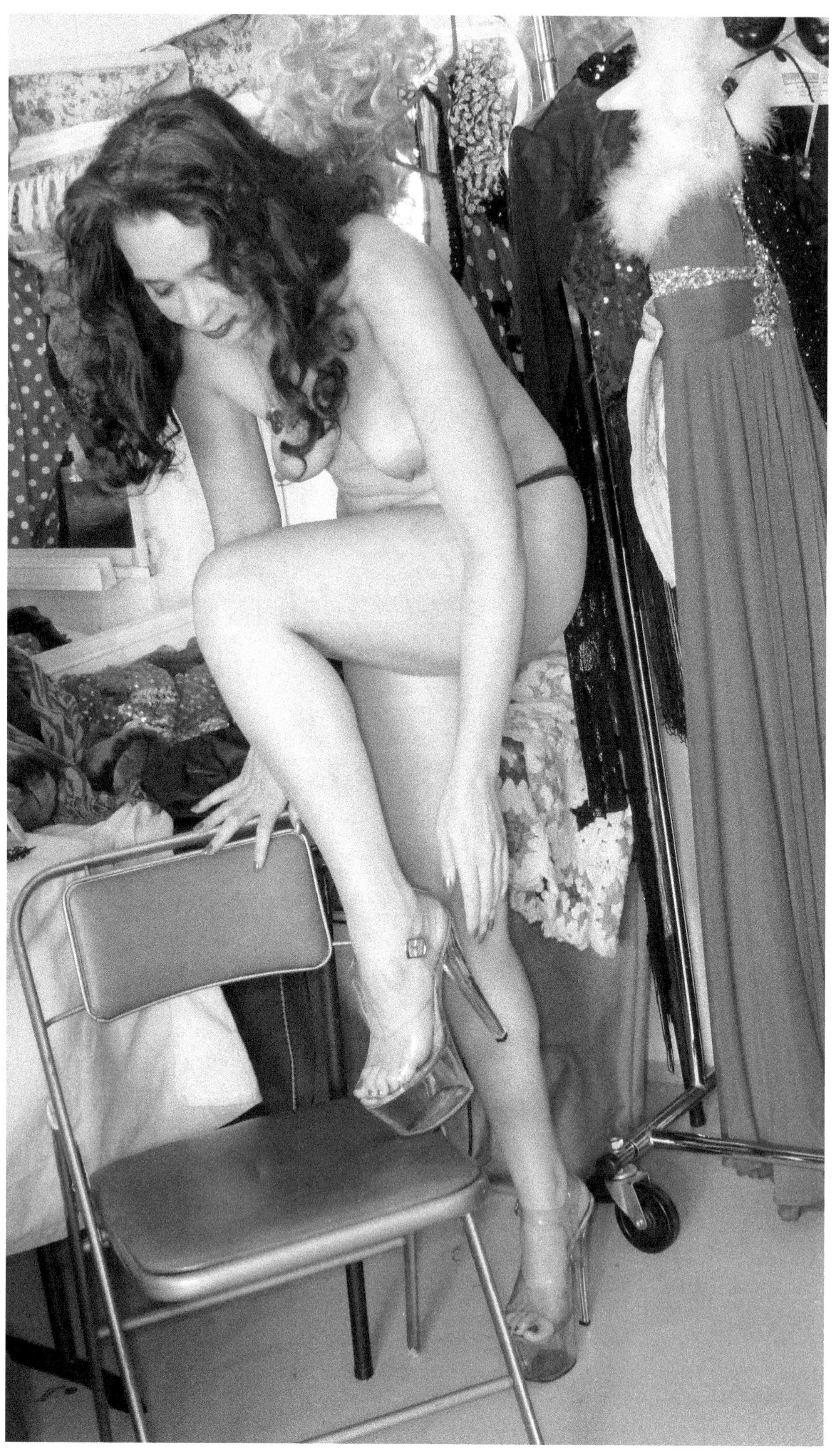

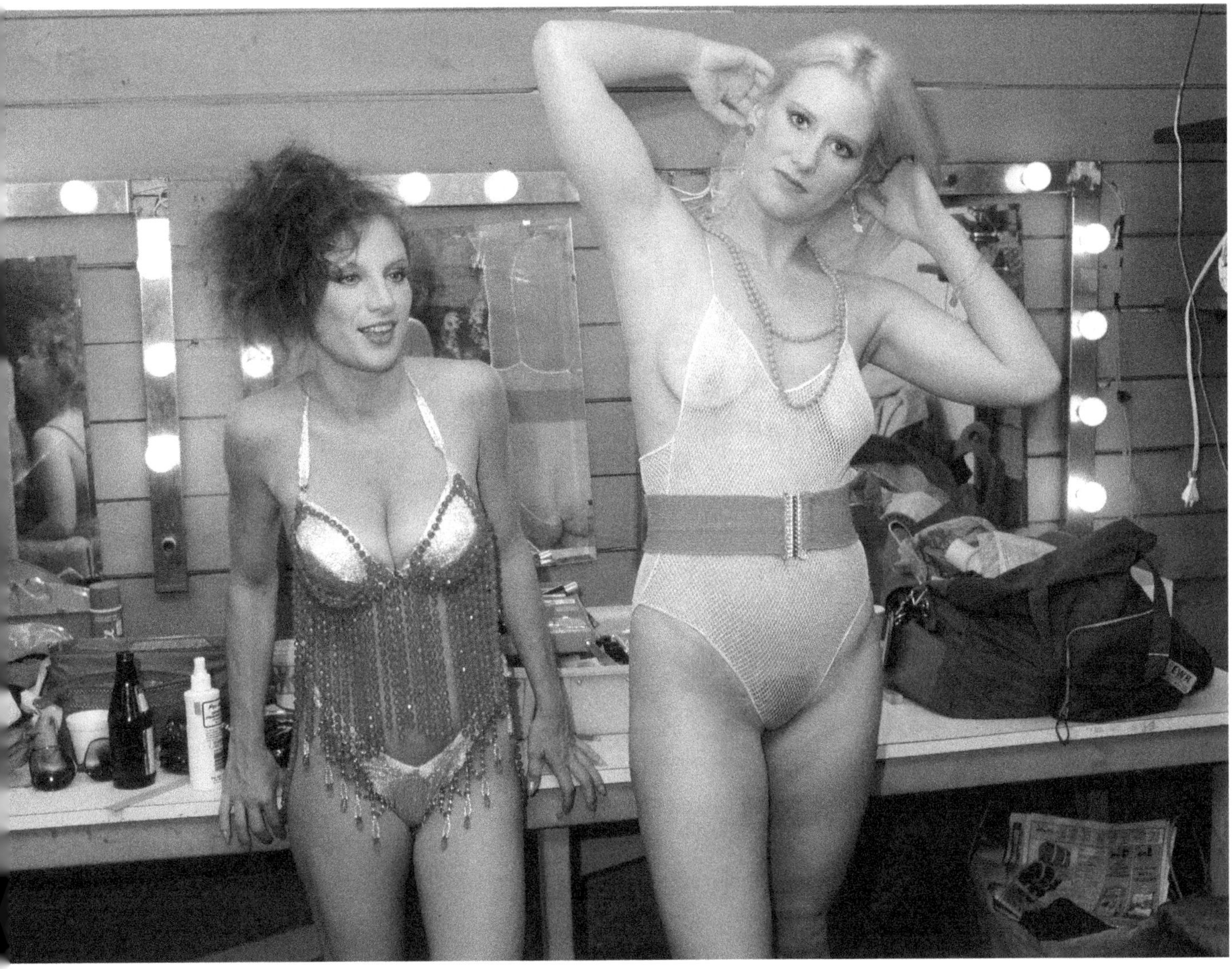

To Be

Backs and breasts.

Backstage bitterness.

Buttocks, bells and bellybuttons.

Being beautiful for big bucks.

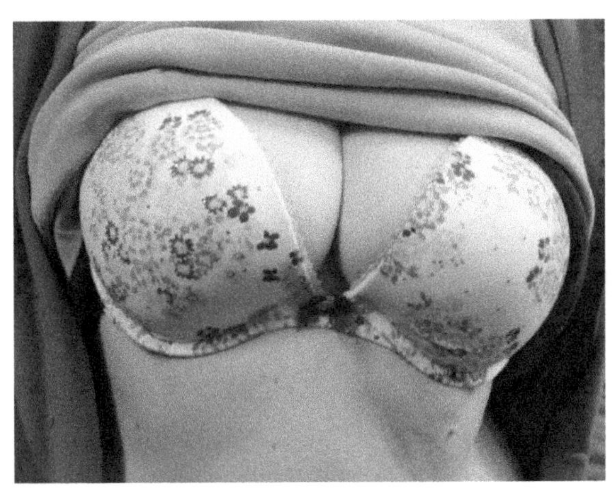

Three Perfumes

Senses:
three perfumes

Sensual:
share a joint.

Adjust a sequined skirt,
dangle legs,
be bored.

Can I borrow
your deodorant?

You wanna have
a drink after work?

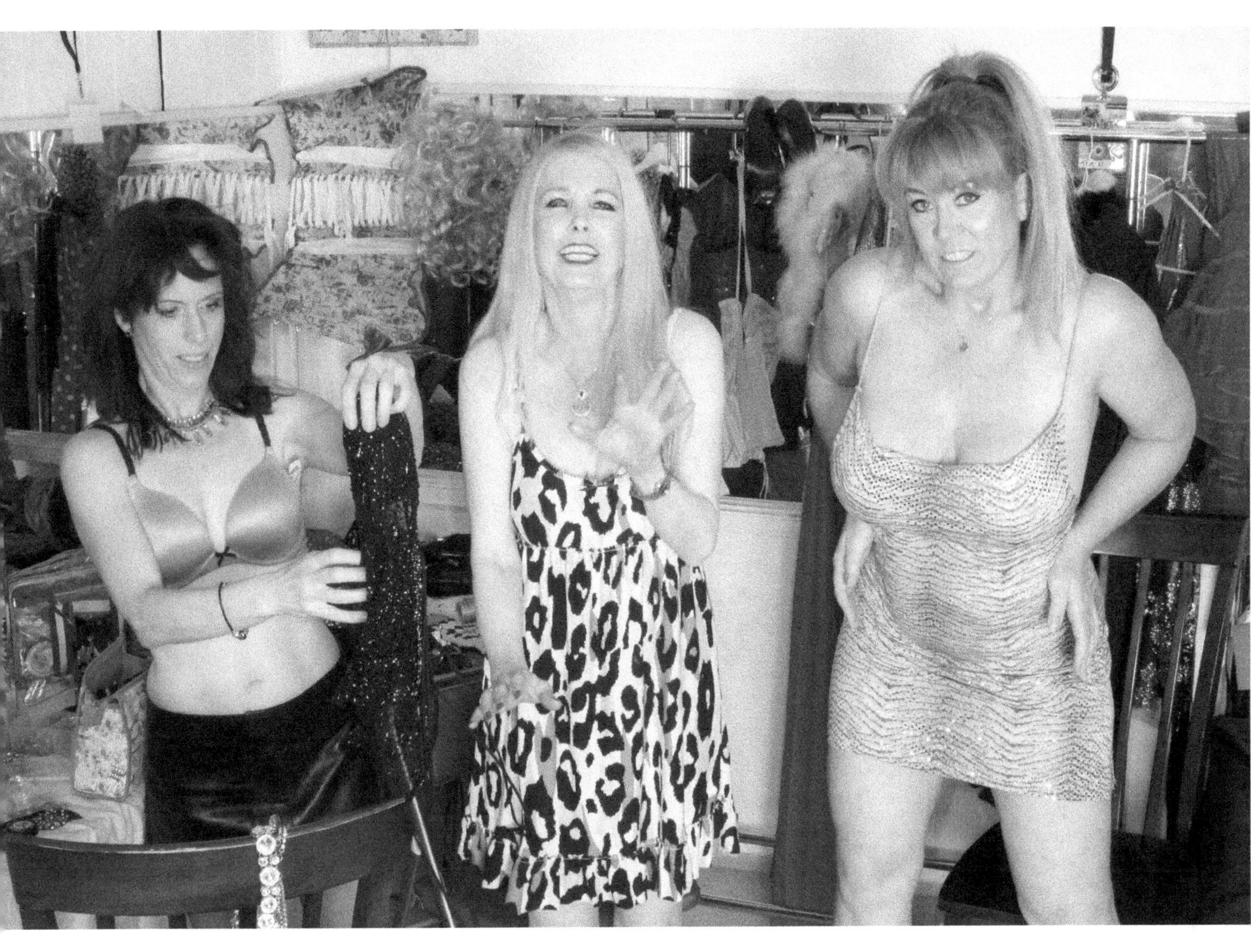

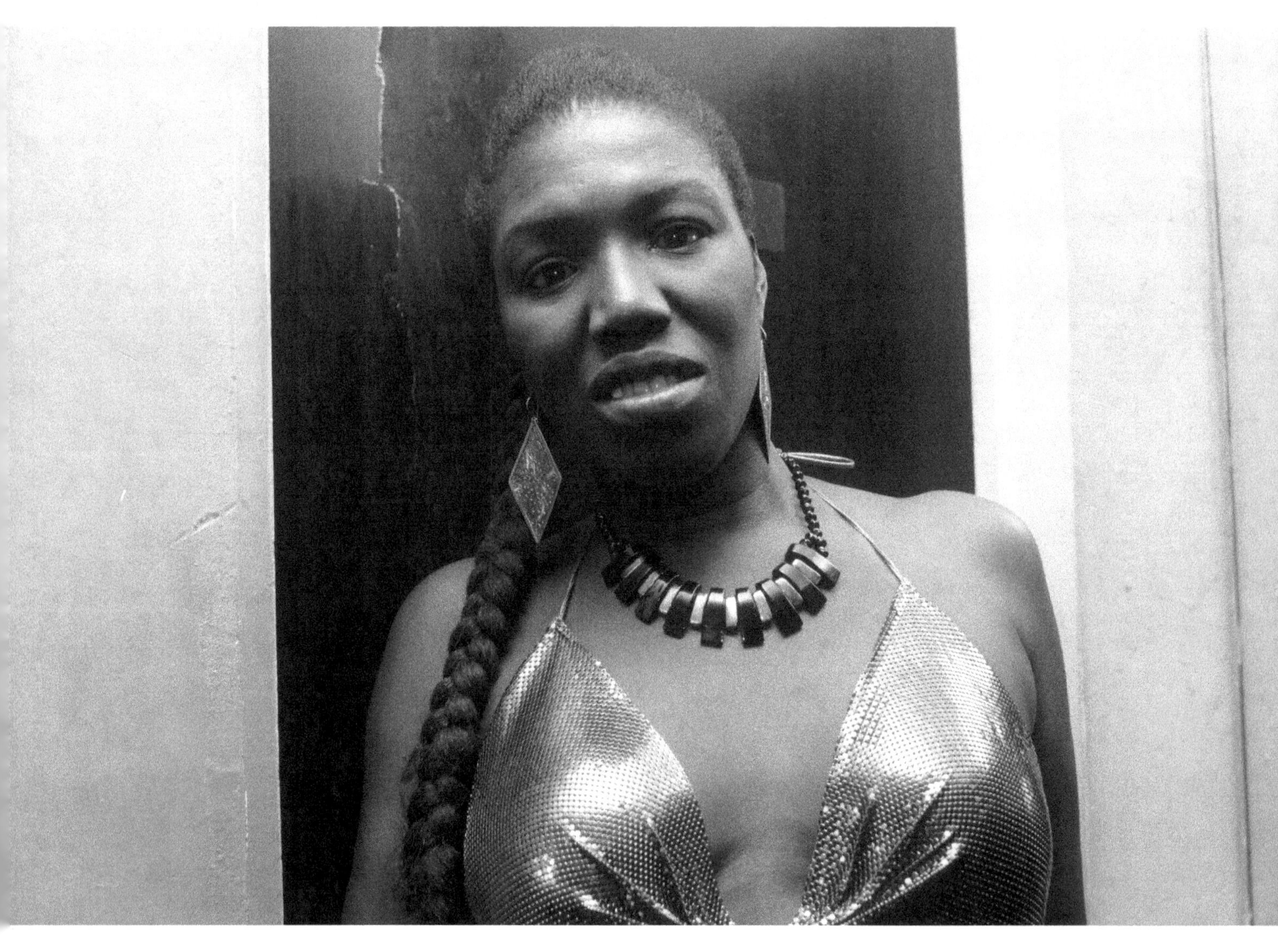

Tanya's Refrain

She is tall.
She is black.

She is.

She is
afraid
and so
lonely.

G-String Nooses

The GANG. Dildoes.
The GIRLS. Paddles.
The LADIES. Kiss.
The DANCERS. Fuck.

Sweat,
cry,
musk.

Dress up in
lacy underwear,
hang themselves in
g-string nooses.

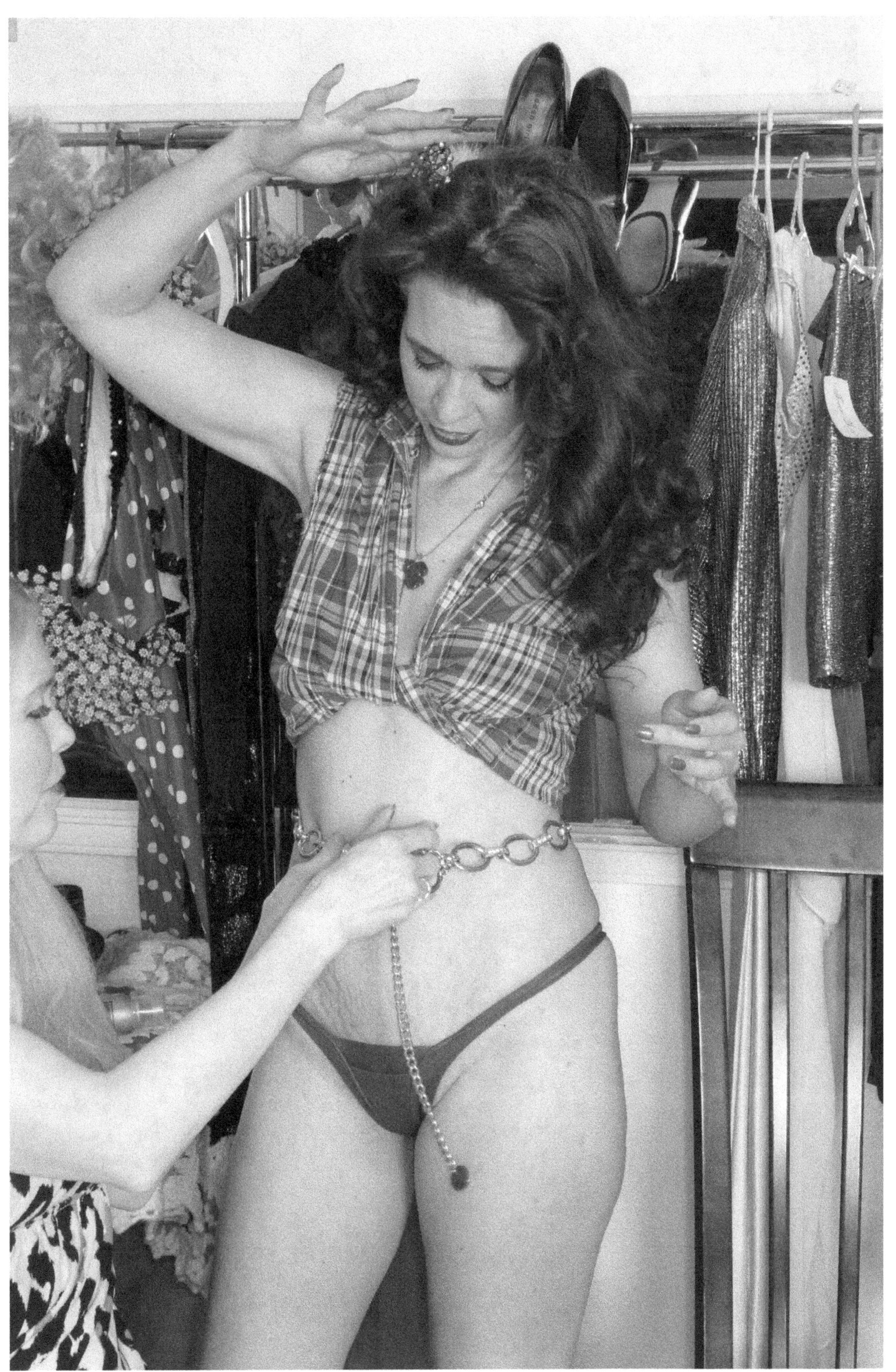

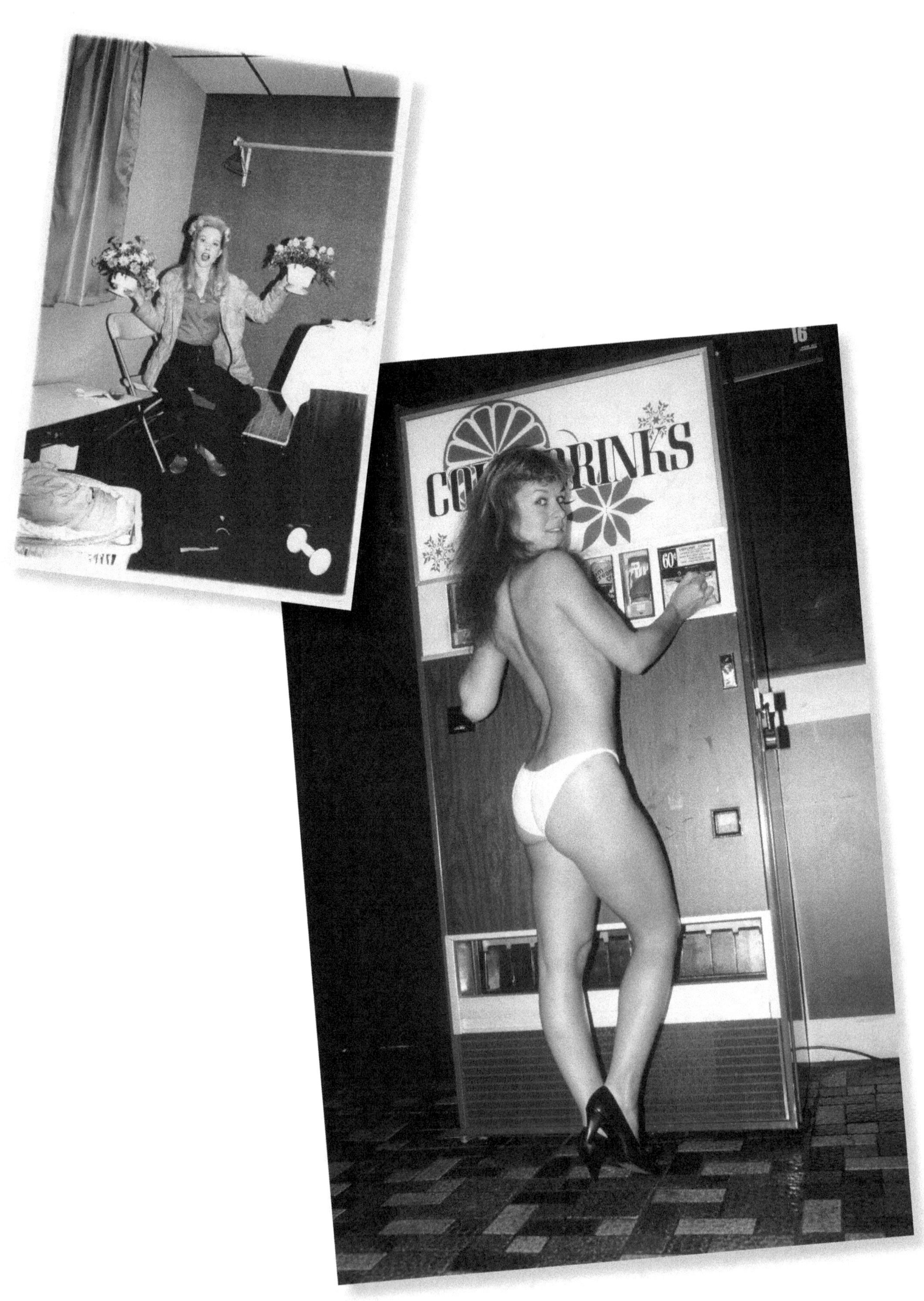

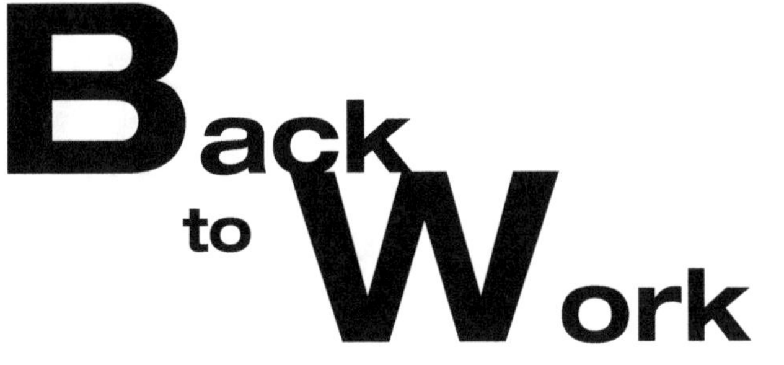

Back to Work

Armpit hair.
Three holes in an ear.
Cheap rings hang.
Flowers were sent.
The phone was yanked out
by the management.
(Too many dope deals.)

Get back to work.

Weary Souls

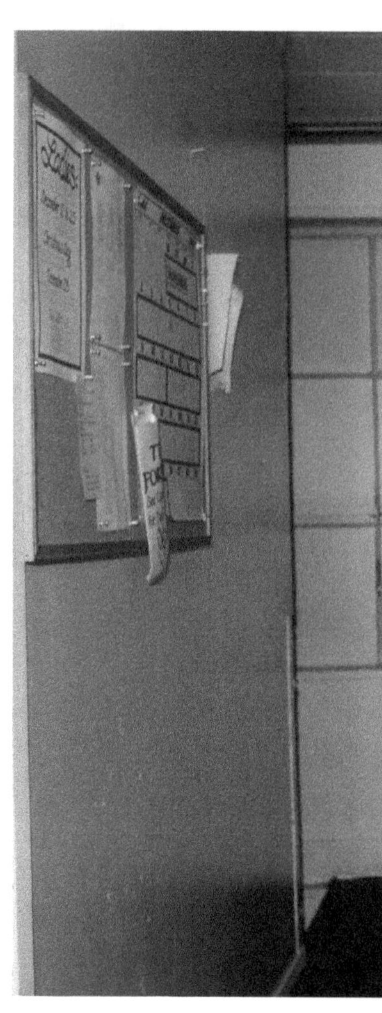

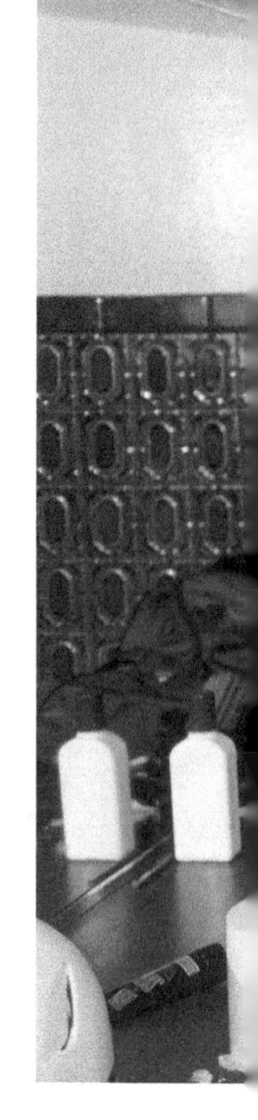

Sorts and shapes,
weary.

Prettying up
to stay up.

Go home
to sleep.

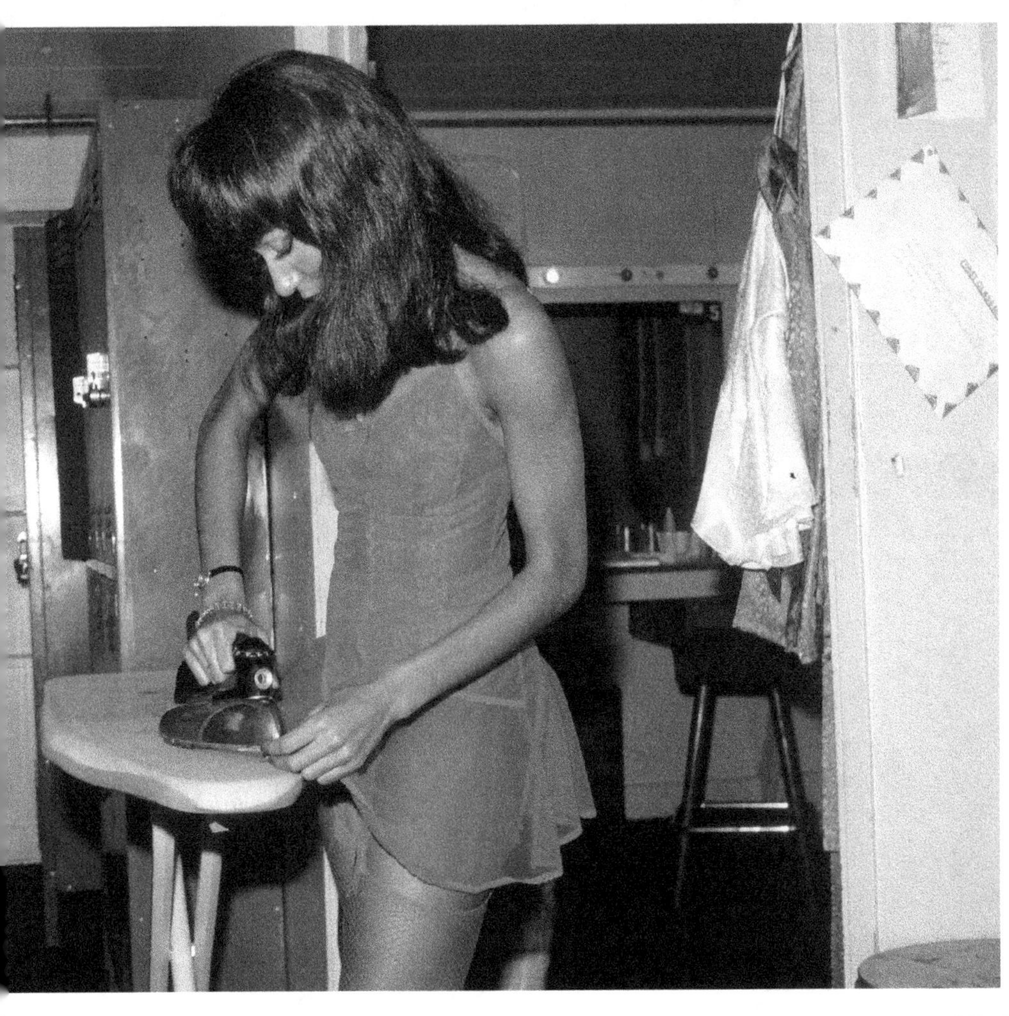

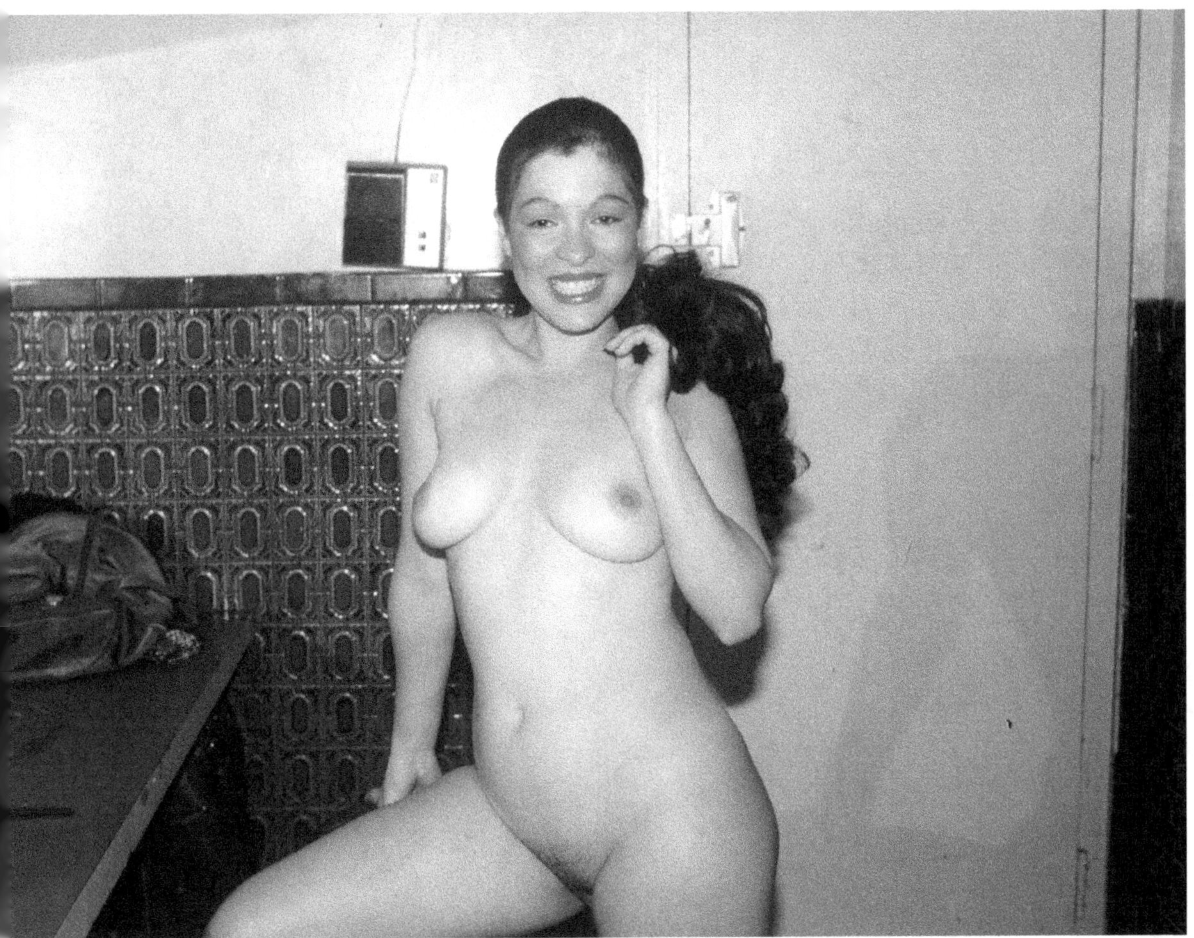

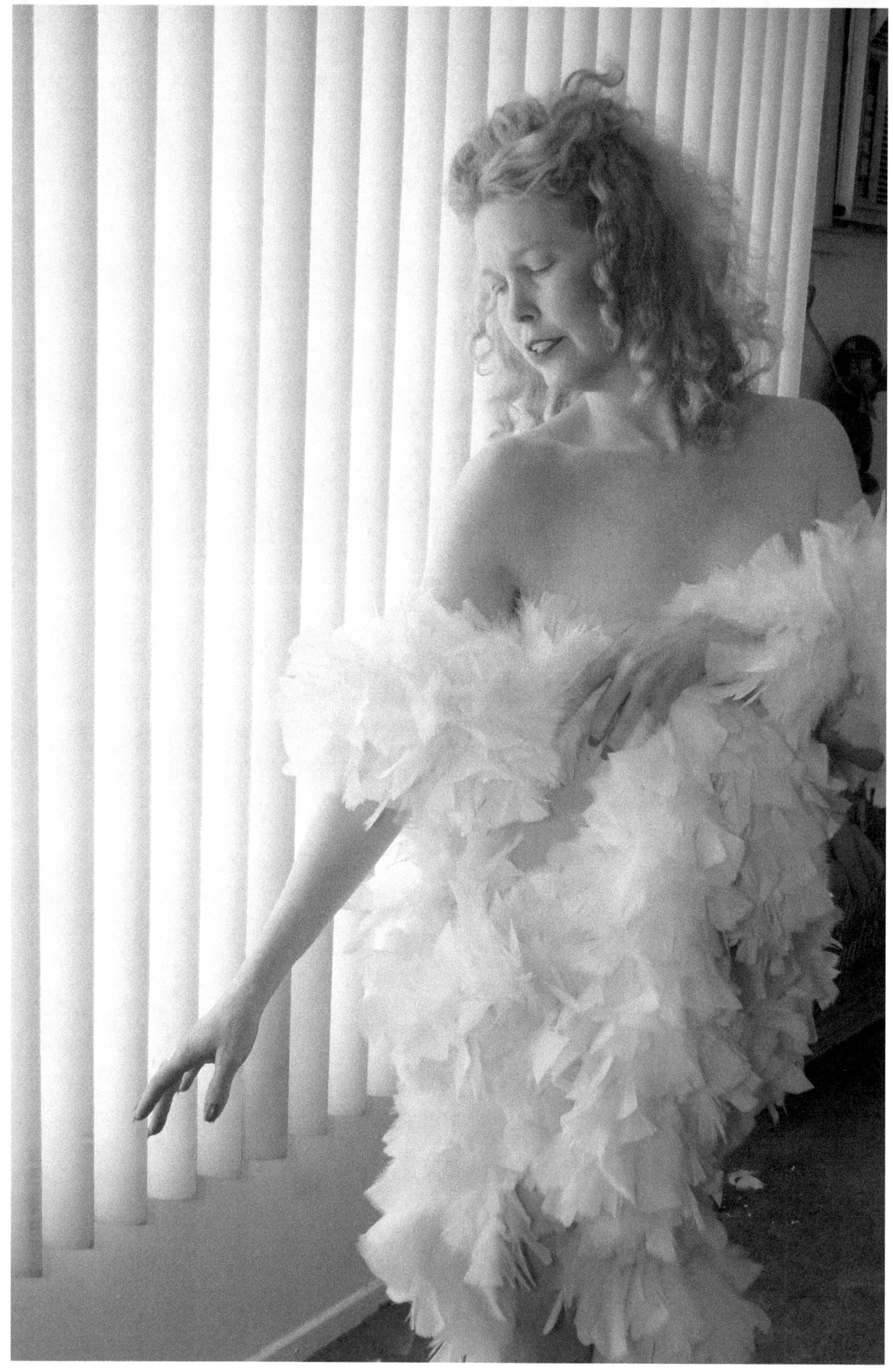

Fog II

Sometimes I think
I'm being followed
down this cold street.
but it is my own footsteps
getting ahead of themselves,
tripping over the foghorn's whistle,
hurrying to meet you
under the kiss of a wet street lamp.

Bright Lights

She told me
if I ever wrote
about her
to say,

"Bright lights,
lonely nights."

That is the truth of her life.

She hasn't been
asked on a real date
in two years.

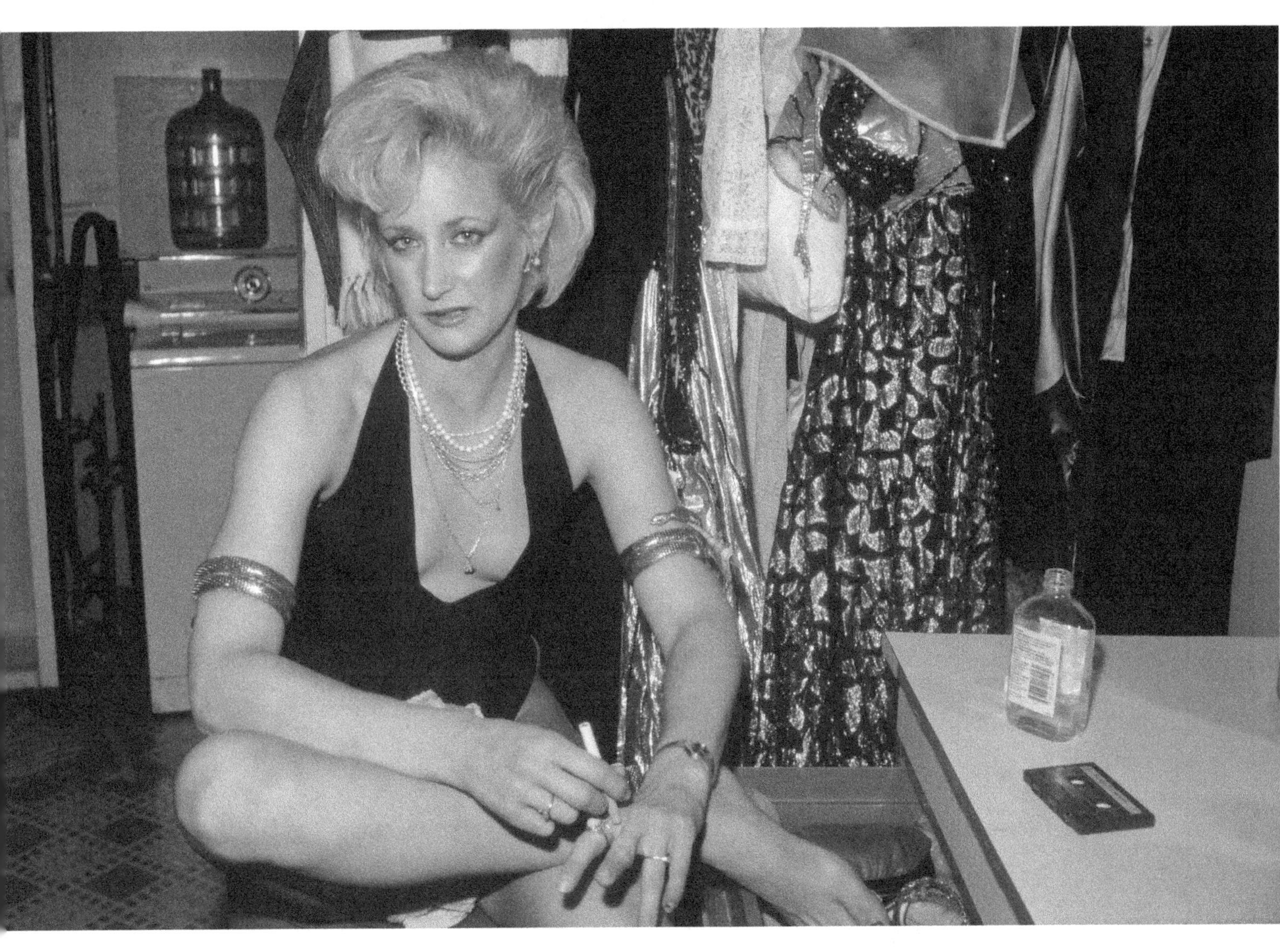

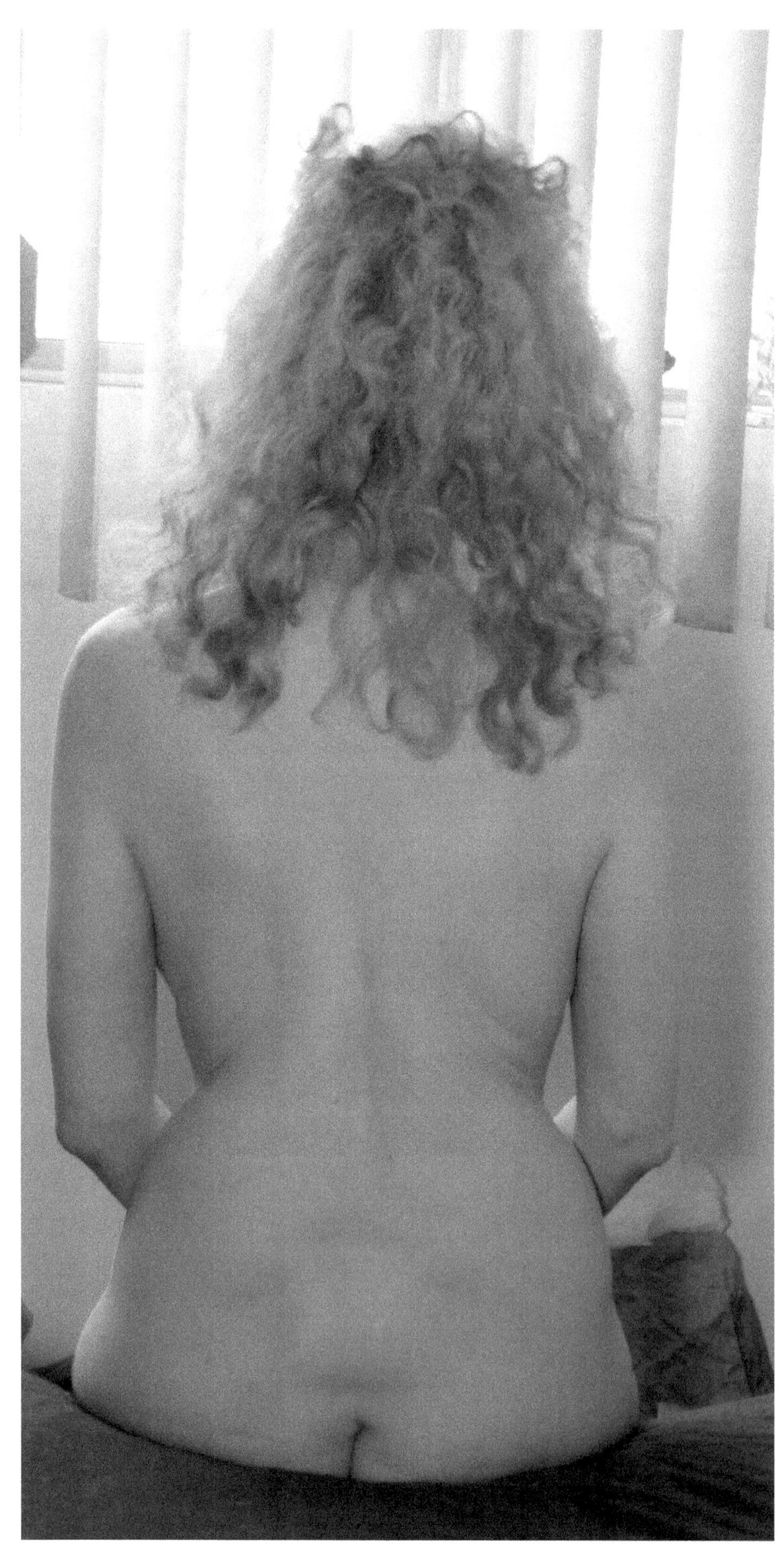

Bodies

Big tits.
Small butts.
Large nipples.
Sore holes
Ripe clits.

Bones and
blood and
a reaching out.

Always coming back
empty.

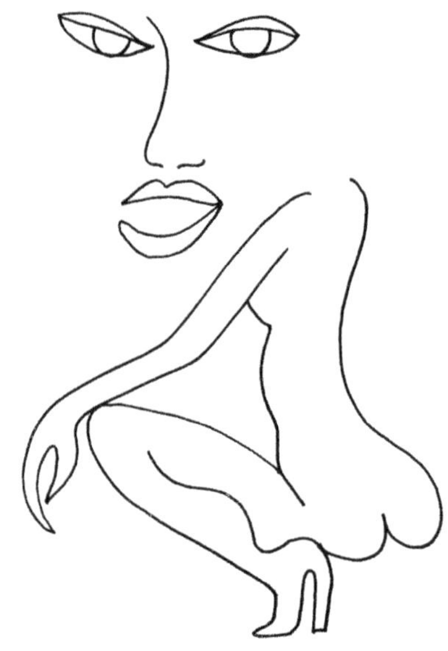

The Drawings

At the theatre, I socialized with the women and took photos of them between my time on stage. I was living with an artist then who encouraged me to also draw what I saw around me.

I did.

The drawings on the following pages are sketches I made, inspired by the Girls Backstage.

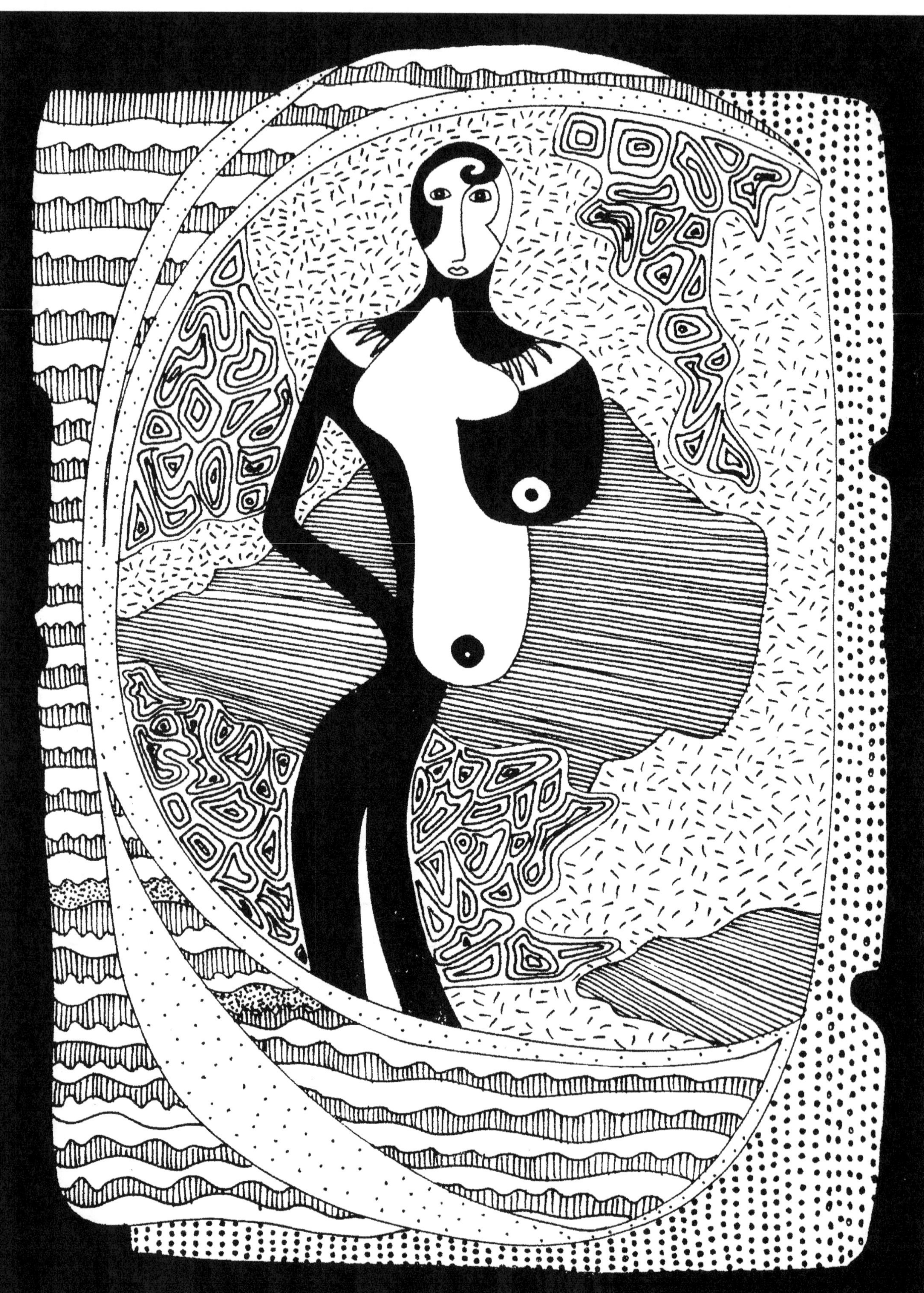

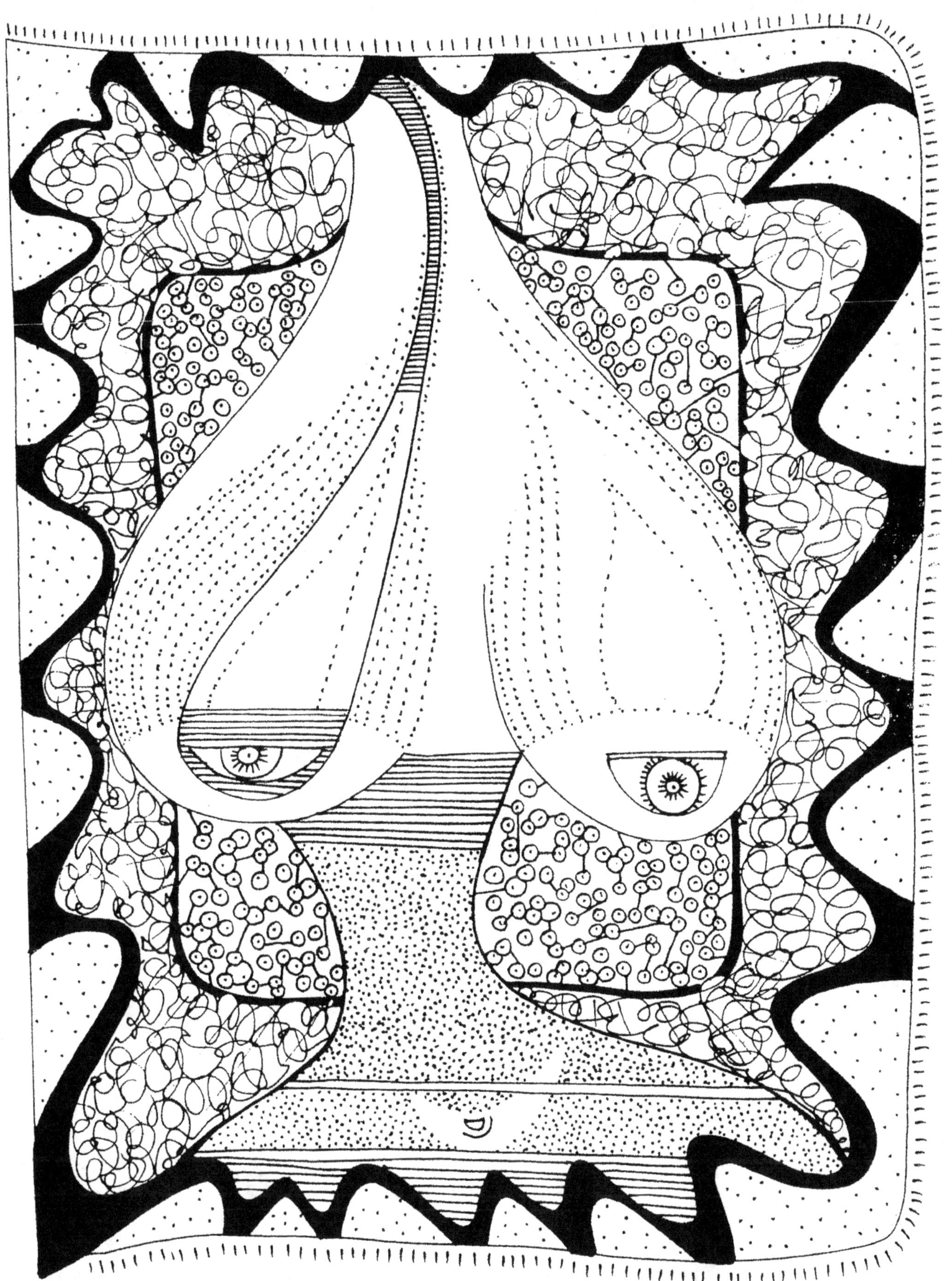

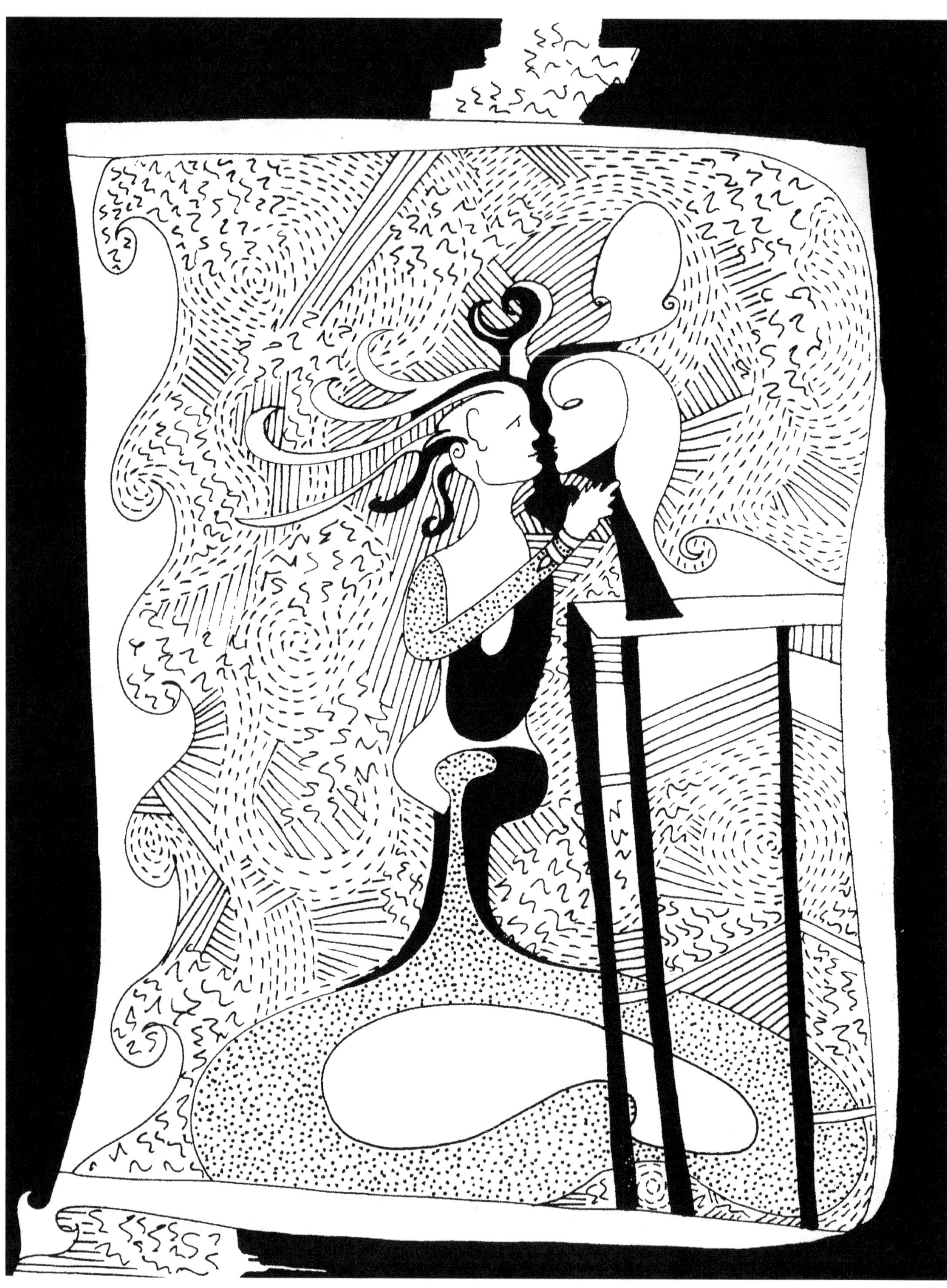

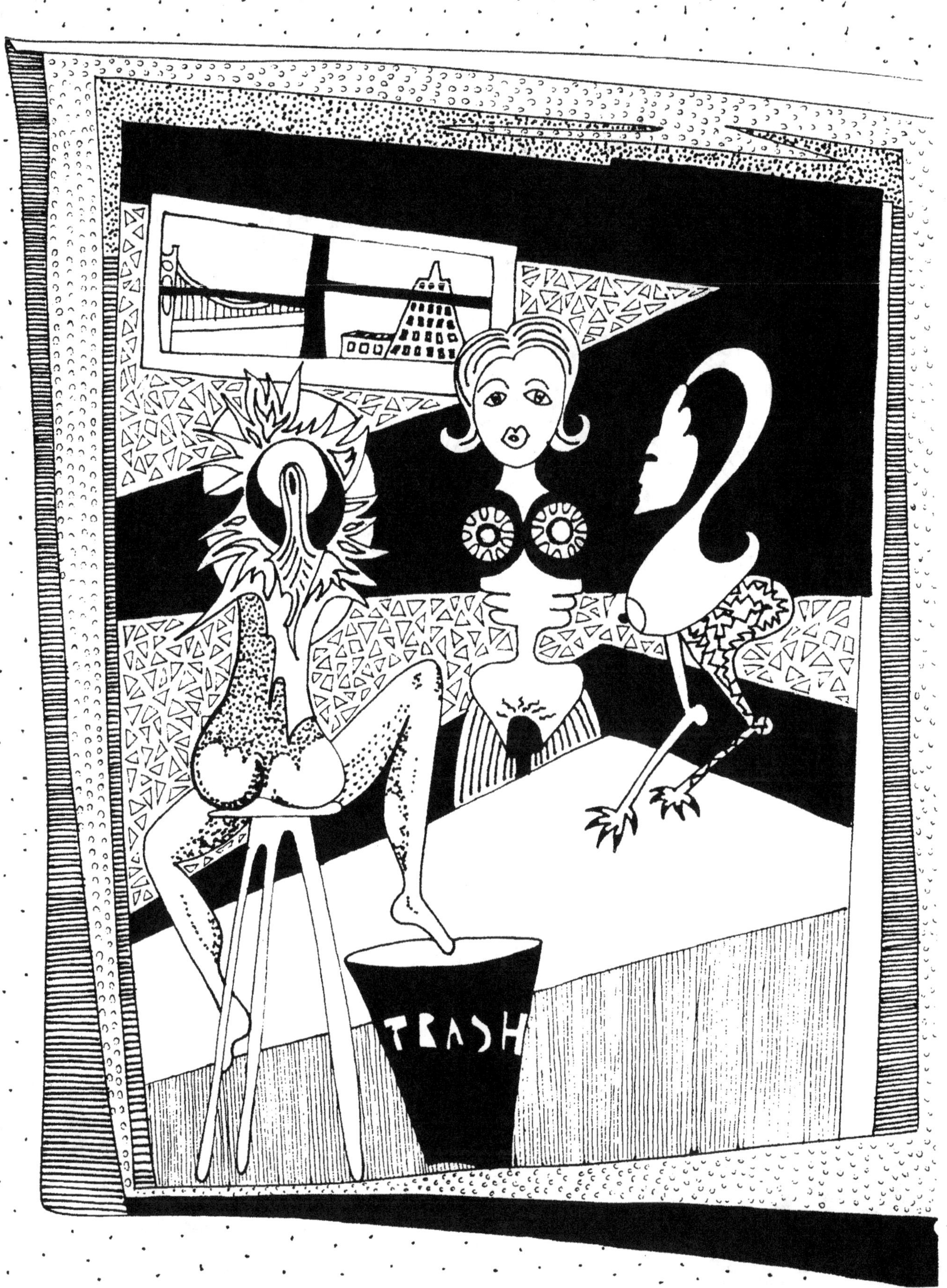
TRASH

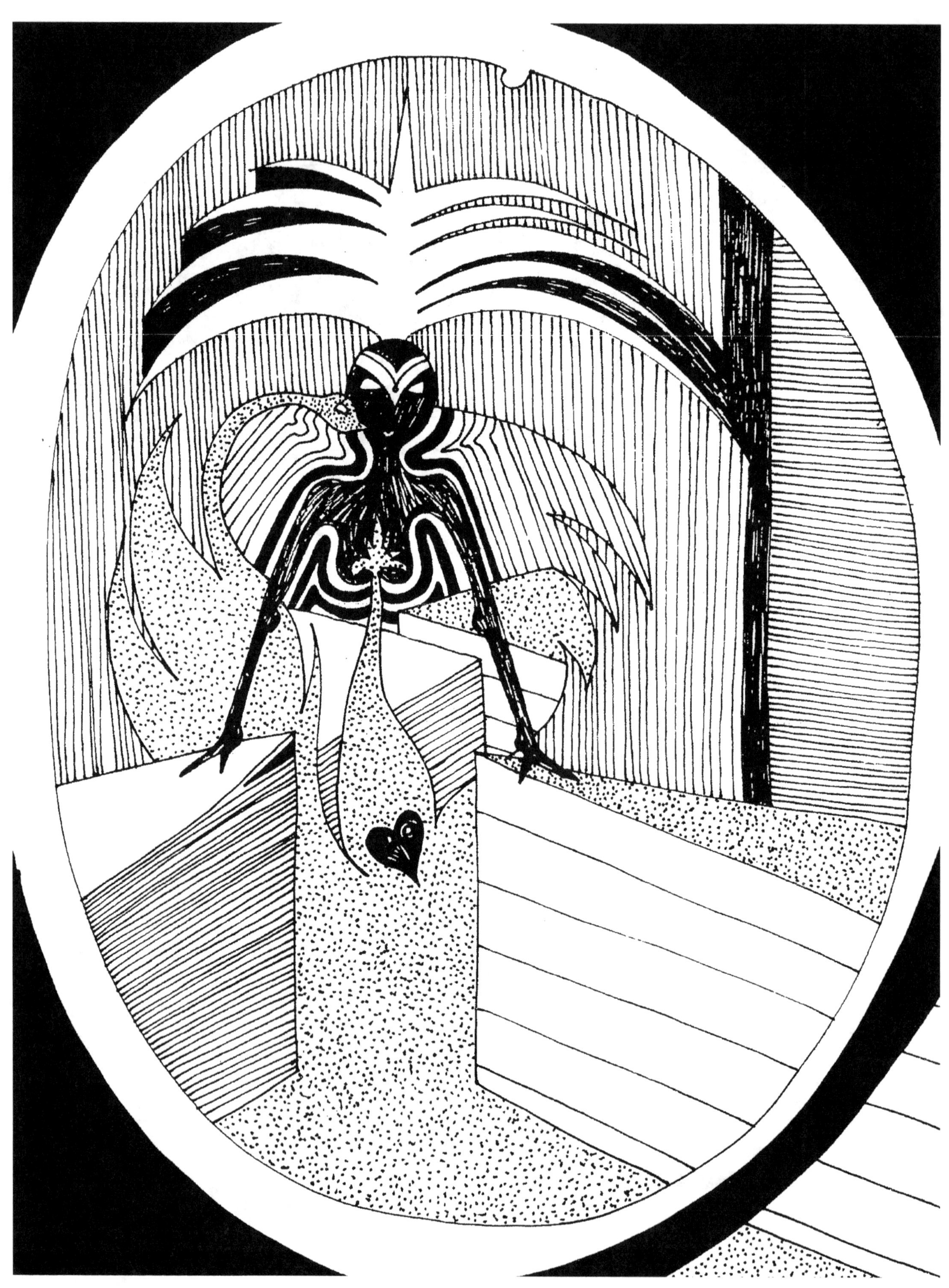

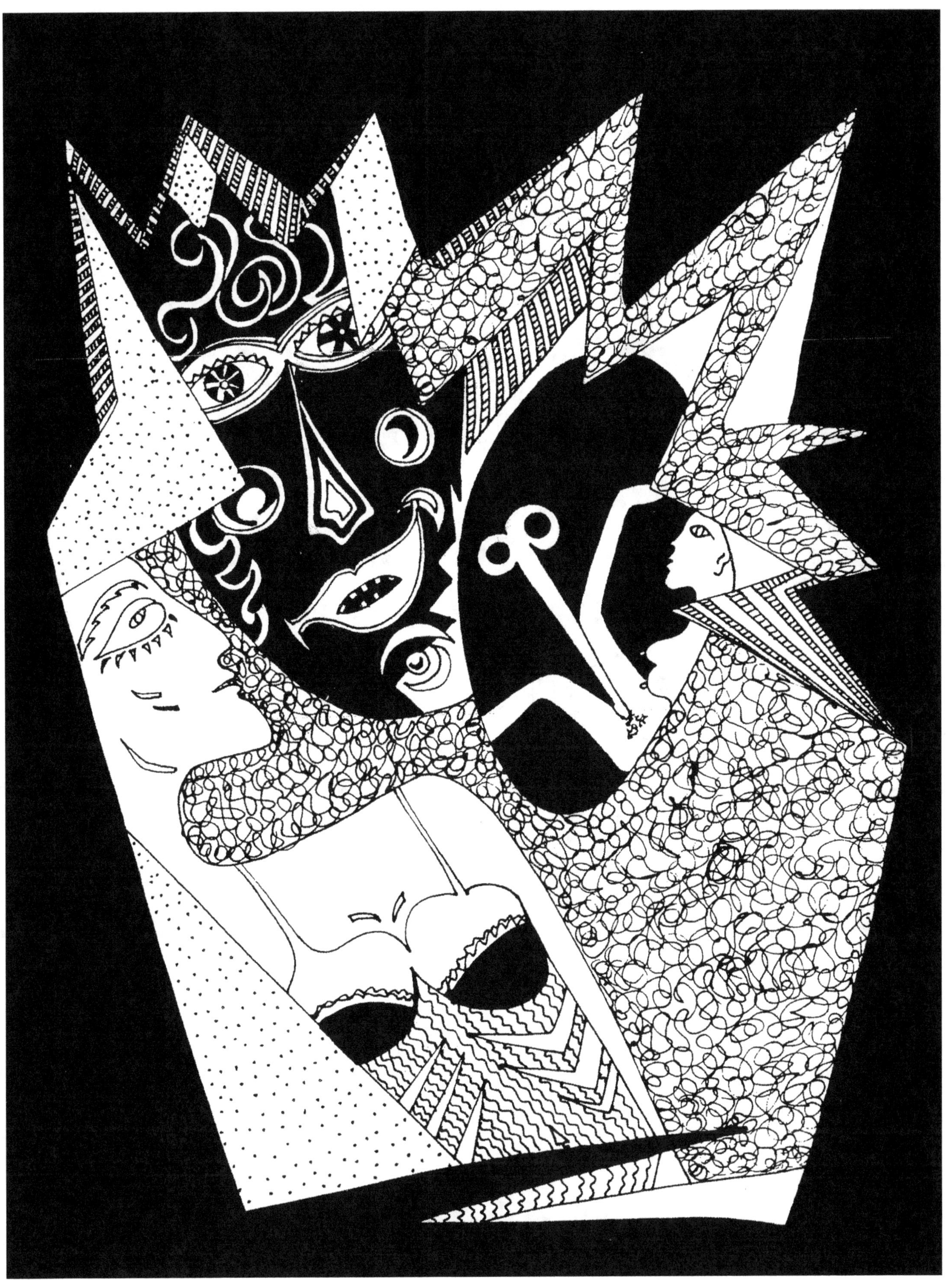

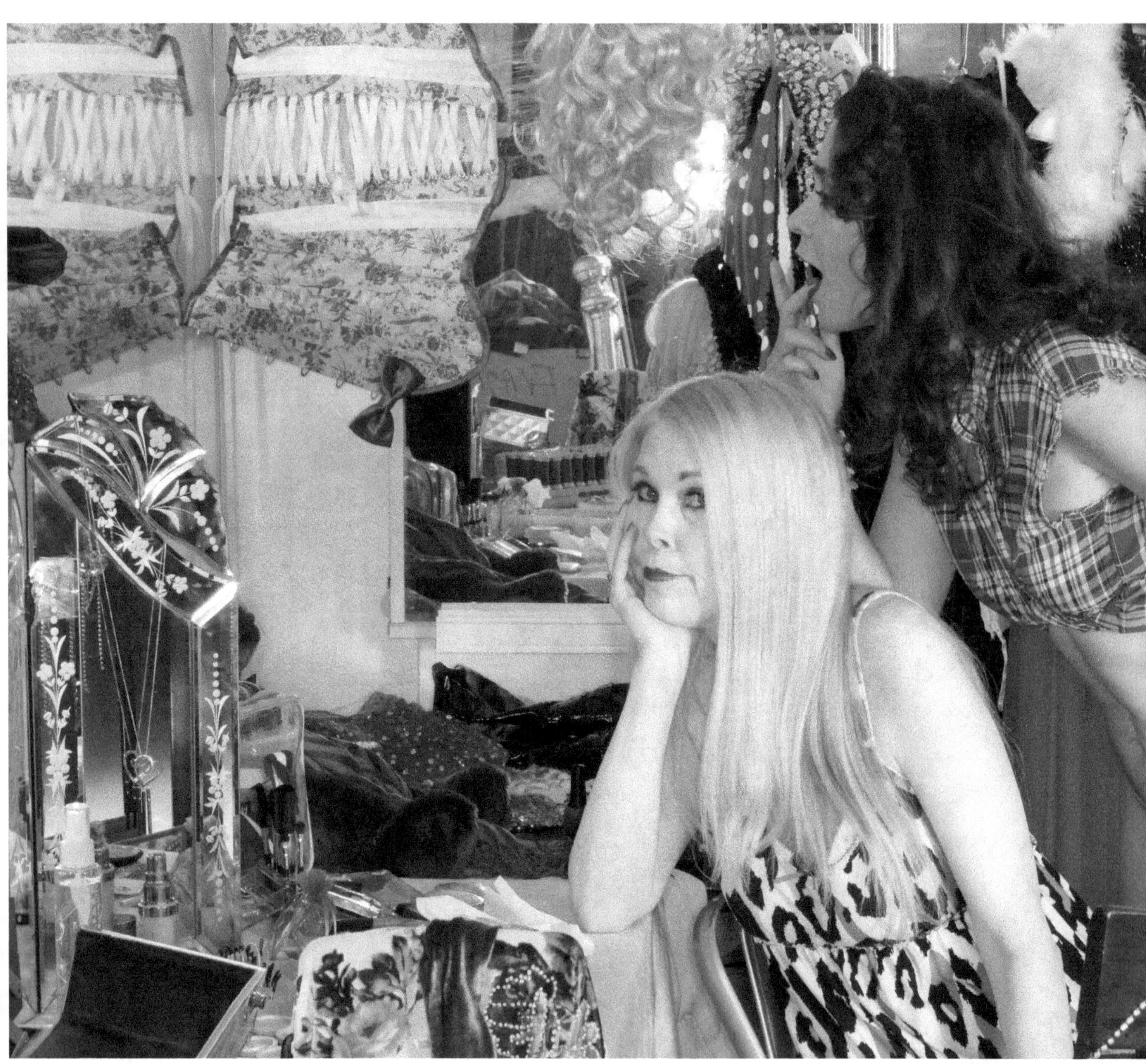

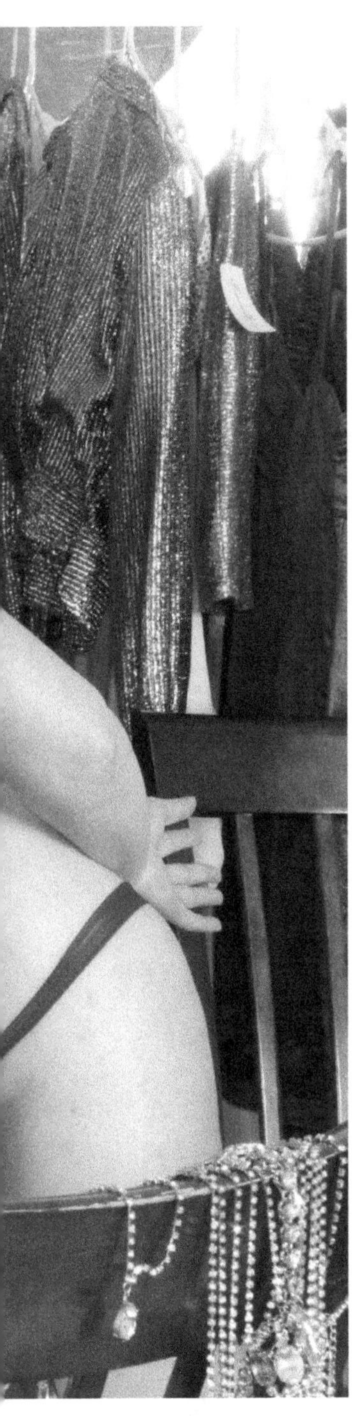

About The Author

Serena Czarnecki is a creative soul at heart—artist, poet, actress, dancer, model and author. A proud, unapologetic bipolar woman, she uses the diverse sexual knowledge she culled as a 1970s porn icon to her advantage. A cornerstone in classic erotic cinema, Serena has been featured in more than 100 adult films like *Sweet Cakes* and *The Ecstasy Girls*. She has appeared in countless men's magazines including *Playboy*, *Penthouse* and *Hustler*.

Serena drew upon her modern dance prowess when she headlined theatres, stripping her way across the United States as an exotic dancer. *Backstage Girls* includes poetic reflections of her time as a feature at the O'Farrell Theatre in San Francisco.

Jill C. Nelson's *Golden Goddesses: 25 Legendary Women of Classic Erotic Cinema 1968-1985* tells more of Serena's vivid career onstage and onscreen. (Serena also graces its cover.) Her memory book *Bright Lights, Lonely Nights* is available from BearManor Bare (bearmanorbare.com).

She's always considered herself a hippie and now lives as a happy hermit in a magical wood on a magical mountain with her soul mate. These days, Serena writes poetry and paints pictures.

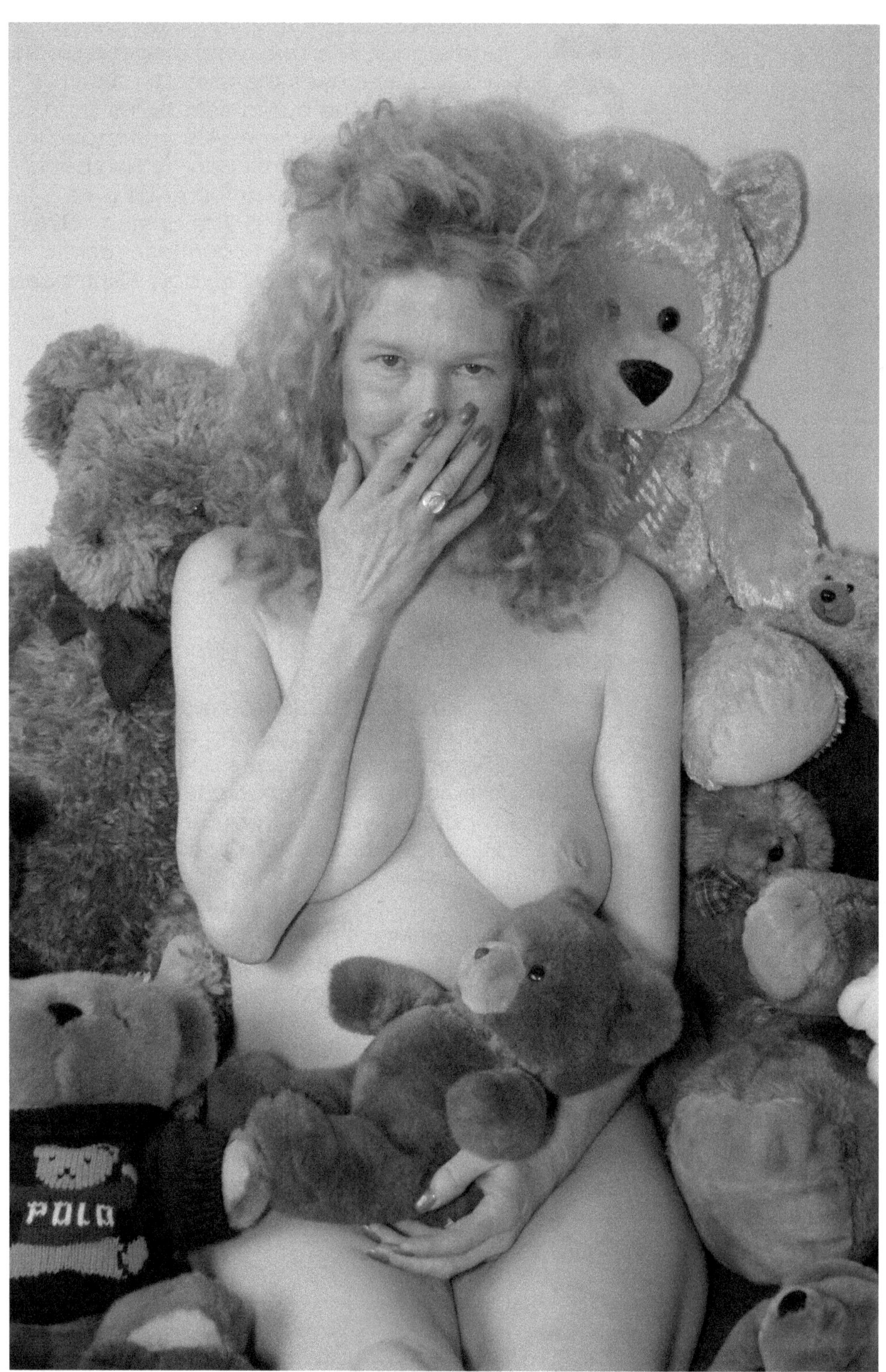
POLO

Special Thanks To:

Karen Summer

Bill Margold

Lady Sable Renae

Bill from Iraq

Traci Cannibal

Melissa Hill

and Joel Sussman

And a heartfelt thanks to:

Phil Johnson,
who archived *Backstage Girls* for many years and encouraged me to put it into a finished form.

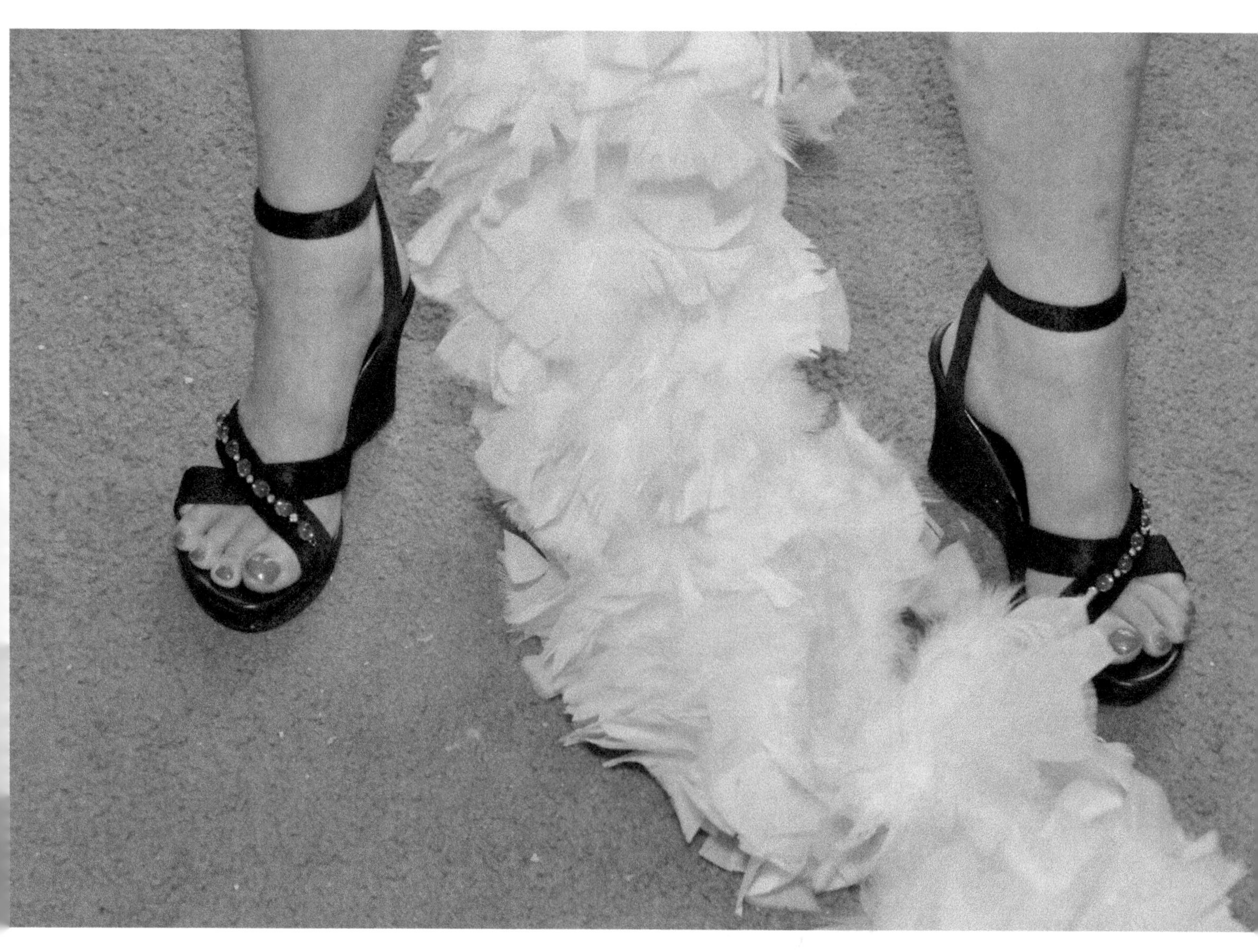

Photo Credits:

Annie Sprinkle: Page 2, 5, 11, 13, 17, 18, 20, 28, 29, 30, 35, 39, 43, 44, 49, 52, 54, 56, 59, 60, 64, 70, 71, 72, 74, 75, 78, 81, 85, 87, 89, 91, 95, 98, 102, 105, 109

Steve Zambrano: Page 6, 7, 9, 13, 23, 24, 27, 33, 34, 37, 47, 48, 55, 63, 67, 77, 82, 90, 93, 94, 97, 101, 106, 110, 120, 122, 124, 126

Serena Czarneck: Page 68

Baron Wolman: Page 14, 40

Paul Johnston: Page 51, 95

From The Estate of Michael Bowen & Serena's Personal Collection: Page 102

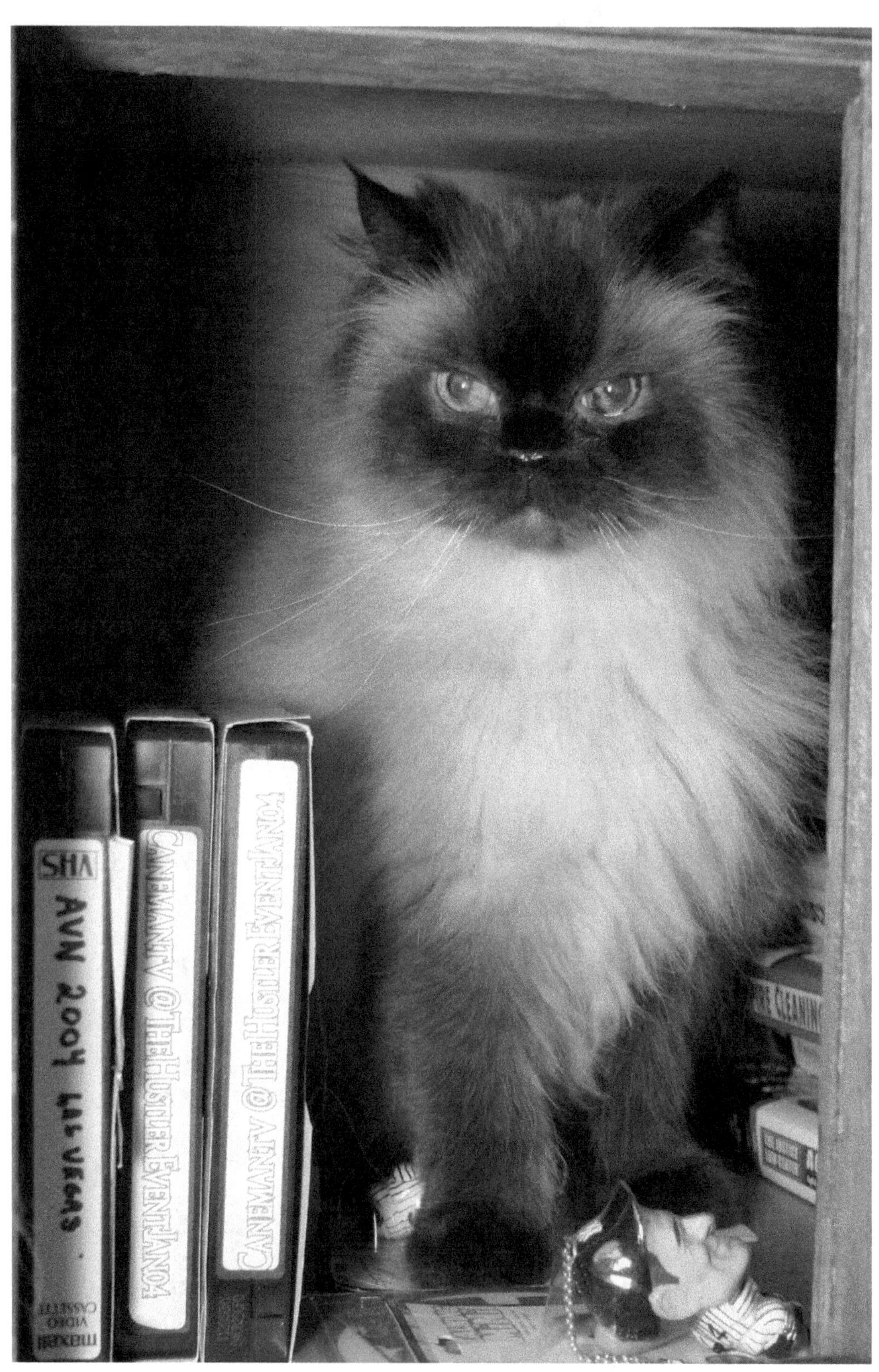
VHS
AVN 2004 LAS VEGAS
maxell VIDEO CASSETTE
CANEMANTV @ THE HUSTLER EVENT JAN 04
CANEMANTV @ THE HUSTLER EVENT JAN 04

About The Other Photographers:

Although I took many of the photographs in ***Backstage Girls****, while I was working on the project, I came across several photographers whose work spoke to me on a visceral level and perfectly captured the exotic dancers' behind-the-scenes world. Some photographers took pictures of me. Some took pictures of others. All were so striking that I wanted to include their work in this book.*

- S.C.

Paul Johnston is a native Californian. He attended three colleges and has worked running bicycle tours, in biotech, building small structures and has spent over ten years growing orchids. He has always taken photographs.

Annie Sprinkle is a former porn star who strut her stuff on the bumpy burlesque trail to put herself through School of Visual Arts in New York City. She morphed into a performance artist and earned a PhD in human sexuality. Currently, she is pollinating the ecosex movement. (sexecology.org)

Baron Wolman was *Rolling Stone Magazine's* first Chief Photographer. His photographic prints are widely collected and his most recent books include *Baron Wolman: The Rolling Stone Years, Groupies*, and *Woodstock*. (fotobaron.com)

Steve Zambrano enjoys the art of documenting behind-the-scenes magic. Serena was in the first erotic art film he ever saw. *Backstage Girls* is his second creative project with her. His work has been published in magazines like *GQ*, newspapers and several books.

Murder

The ad in *The Daily* tells all I've arrived.
I will headline the O'Farrell for a week.

The money is good; the girls sweet.
The brothers treat me nice at first—
until just too much cocaine
makes them crazy.

Shots ring out in the chaos
and someone is killed.
Cain and Able all over again.

I'm out of town dancing for
other men, other bosses.
Dancing, twirling,
taking off my clothes happily.

It is years before I hear of the murder.
And when I do, I know who is dead
and who's in prison.

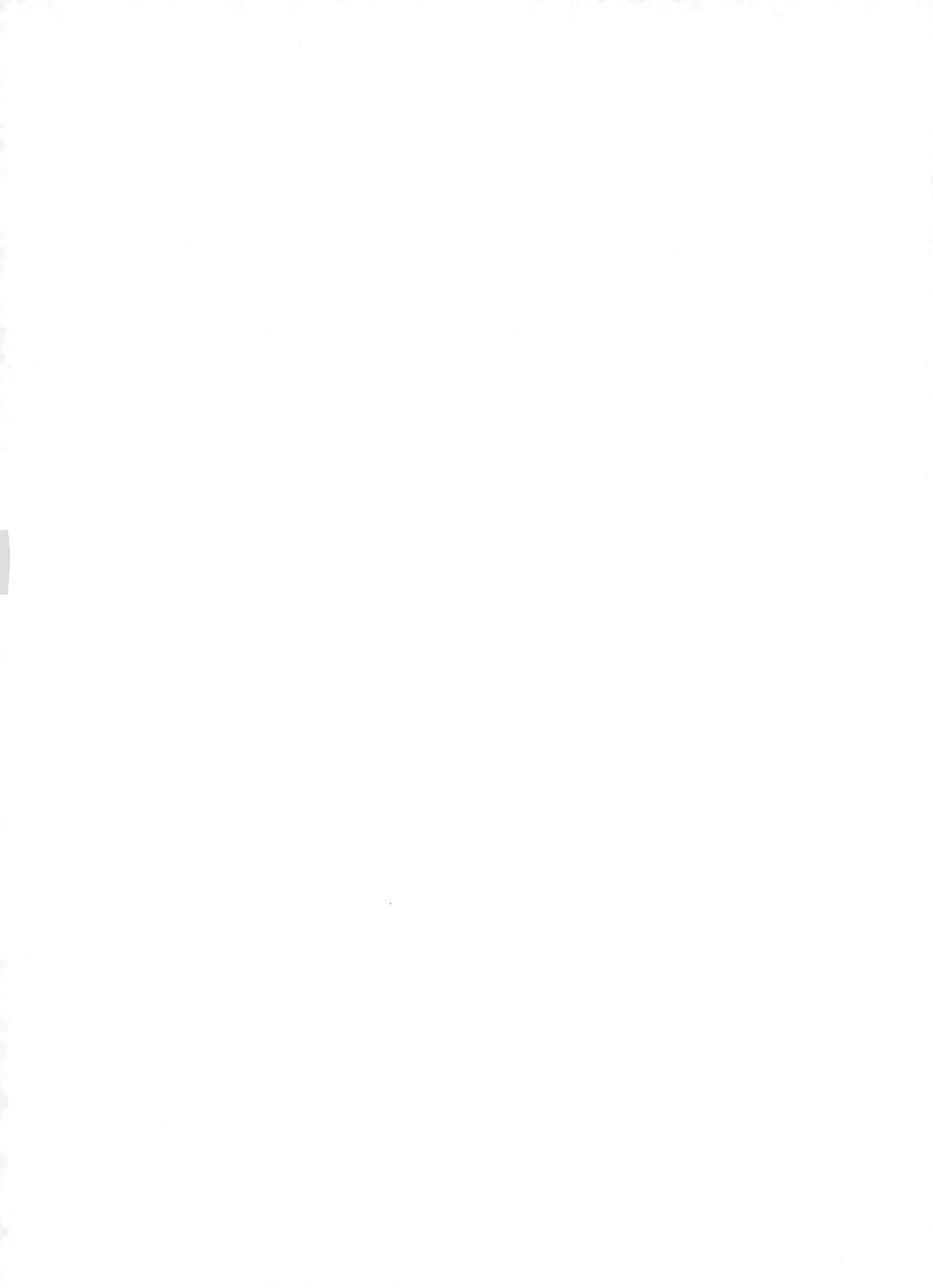

www.ingramcontent.com/pod-product-compliance
Lightning Source LLC
LaVergne TN
LVHW081527100826
845153LV00003B/221

* 9 7 8 0 9 9 9 6 9 1 6 6 3 *